Parenting the Overactive Child

PARENTING THE OVERACTIVE CHILD

Alternatives to Drug Therapy

Dr. Paul Lavin

Madison Books
Lanham • New York • London

Copyright © 1989 by

Paul Lavin

Madison Books

4720 Boston Way
Lanham, MD 20706

3 Henrietta Street
London WC2E 8LU England

British Cataloging in Publication Information Available

Library of Congress Cataloging-in-Publication Data

Lavin, Paul.
Parenting the overactive child : alternatives to drug therapy / Paul Lavin.
p.   cm.
Bibliography: p.
1. Hyperactive children.   2. Parenting.   I. Title
RJ506.H9L38   1989   649'.153—dc20   89–2613 CIP

ISBN 0–8191–7297–9 (alk. paper)
ISBN 0–8191–7315–0 (pbk.: alk. paper)

All Madison Books are produced on acid-free paper.
The paper used in this publication meets the minimum requirements of American
National Standard for Information Sciences—Permanence of Paper for Printed Library
Materials, ANSI Z39.48–1984.   ∞

Contents

Introduction

This book is about rearing children who are diagnosed as having Attention Deficit Hyperactivity Disorder (ADHD). As a practicing child psychologist and university professor over the past seventeen years, I have become increasingly more concerned about the over-prescription of stimulant medication in treating these youngsters. In writing this text, I present other alternatives that have been used successfully with ADHD children. I believe these methods are safer and provide better training for these youngsters in acquiring self-control and a more positive self-image. Essentially, I have tried to develop an instructional package for parents that actively integrates current research and clinical information that can be applied in rearing ADHD children.

The emphasis of the book is directed toward providing guidance to parents of children who range in age from two to twelve. It is during these years that parents have maximum influence on their youngster's development. Parents who effectively use their knowledge about child rearing at this time are more likely to positively influence character formation and prepare their youngsters to succeed in the future. Thus, the purpose of this book is to provide various approaches that can be applied with ADHD children in this age range.

1

In each of the chapters I provide parents with specific techniques to be used in assisting their ADHD child to develop those personality characteristics essential to responsible and productive living. Basically, I have made concrete suggestions that will help parents to shape and mold the child's behavior. I have focused on methods that parents can utilize to promote the child's development of a sensible, realistic philosophy about life. Specific techniques are presented to parents for increasing their youngster's self-awareness and teaching him or her to more effectively cope with life's challenges. In the appendixes I have provided additional lists of suggestions and readings. These can be used to make the contents of the text even more practical as a guide in rearing the ADHD child.

Finally, I would like to stress that there is no shortcut to successfully rearing ADHD children to be responsible, productive adults. The methods described in this text take time and consistent application if they are to produce the desired results. Being the parent of an ADHD child is not easy. It demands commitment and effort. However, if parents are willing to work diligently, the likelihood of these children developing into happy, successful persons will be increased. Certainly contributions made by parents to the development of their children as coping, integrated adults can be a considerable source of pride and satisfaction.

Chapter 1

Diagnosis: Symptoms and Causes of Hyperactivity

Diagnostic Labels and Symptoms

The diagnosis of hyperactivity is usually made by the family pediatrician. Often this occurs after a child has entered school. The teacher may inform the parents that their child is behaving poorly in the classroom and on the playground. He or she may be inattentive, impulsive, and disruptive. With the parents' permission, the school will forward a checklist and/or a description of the child's behavior to the pediatrician. This information, in conjunction with a history of the child's development, is used to make the diagnosis.

Hyperactivity has been given a variety of names in the past. Hyperkinesis, minimal brain damage, minimal brain dysfunction, and maturational lag are some of the terms associated with this disorder. More recently, the American Psychiatric Association used Attention Deficit Disorder with Hyperactivity as the diagnostic label for overactive children (Diagnostic and Statistical Manual III, 1980). In 1987 the diagnostic term was again changed to Attention Deficit Hyperactivity Disorder (Diagnostic and Statistical Manual III-R, 1987).

Whatever the diagnostic term, hyperactive youngsters engage in a number of behavioral deviations and excesses over a long period of time. Behavioral deviations are actions that are developmentally inappropriate for a youngster's given age level. For example, a ten-year-old child who wets the bed would be behaving atypically in comparison to other youngsters of the same age. Behavioral excesses, in comparison, are of two types. First, hyperactive children overreact. This often occurs when the child faces even minimally frustrating or challenging situations. Instead of calmly trying to solve the problem or asking for help, the youngster lashes out against the person or object that is the source of frustration. The second behavioral excess is the continuation of activity even though restraint or discontinuance would be more appropriate. For example, the child continues to keep talking although everyone else is quietly trying to listen to a concert or a speaker. Hyperactive children usually consistently display a variety of behavioral deviations and excesses. In the following discussion, behavioral deviations and excesses—and their symptoms—are discussed separately.

Behavioral Deviations

Behavioral deviations, as indicated previously, are actions developmentally inappropriate for a given child's age level. These deviations can be categorized into the following five groups: (1) Distractibility, inattention, and inability to concentrate; (2) Poor organization; (3) Impulsivity; (4) Poor social skills and self-centeredness; and (5) Failure to plan ahead and a disregard for consequences. Each of these categories will now be discussed separately.

Distractibility, Inattention, and Inability To Concentrate

These symptoms, which frequently occur in school, are readily apparent in the ADHD child. For example, the child fails to sustain effort in the completion of classroom assignments. Sometimes the child begins to work but then starts daydreaming, appearing to be off in space. (In fact, classmates may call the child a "space cadet.") He or she is frequently distracted by sights and sounds both in and outside of the classroom. For example, a bird perched on a window, the sound of an automobile, or a child passing in the hall will temporarily command the youngster's attention. Whereas other children can ignore these, ADHD children cannot block them out. Their attention flits from one thing to another. Often the child does not follow directions. The youngster may forget to put his or her name, the date, or other essential information on the paper. The ADHD child cannot seem to stick to the task at hand. If the work is finished, it is usually messy and inaccurate.

Poor Organization

The ADHD child is poorly organized. School materials are in constant disarray. Books, papers, and pencils are often misplaced or lost. His or her notebook is incomplete and contains crumpled, messy papers that are purposelessly jammed into the binder. Homework assignments are written everywhere except in the assignment notebook.And then they are often written incompletely or inaccurately. If the child does the homework, it gets lost between home and school. (Sometimes the youngster even forgets to turn it in.) Lost homework, books, or supplies may turn up several days later often found in some inappropriate place such as under a bed, behind a door, or in some obscure corner of the house. The child never seems to know how or why this occurred.

Impulsivity

The impulsive child often blurts out a response before the teacher even has a chance to complete the question. Or he or she rushes into an assignment without reading the directions and then can't understand why the work is inaccurate. ADHD youngsters may constantly interrupt other people. It never dawns on them that they are still talking. Rather, the child is in a big hurry to make sure he or she is heard. The child may inadvertently bump into people rushing down the hall to be the first in line. The child doesn't seem to be able to stop from acting quickly even though this irritates other people.

Poor Social Skills, Self-Centeredness

Unfortunately, ADHD children are often disliked by peers. When playing games, they fail to follow the rules, they push ahead of others, or they may actually change or interpret the rules to suit themselves. Sometimes they become overly aggressive in enforcing the rules to obtain an advantage. ADHD children may bully others to get their way. They do not take the rights or feelings of others into consideration. Their own desires and needs are of primary concern. Typically, ADHD children blame others when difficulties arise. They fail to acknowledge any responsibility for contributing to the problem. Rather, it is always caused by someone else. He or she is never at fault. Obviously, such a child has few, if any, friends.

Failure to Plan Ahead, A Disregard for Consequences

ADHD children engage in reckless, dangerous behavior. They do not think about the possible harm they might inflict on themselves or others. For example, Andy may jump from a high place and injure himself when he lands on concrete. Or he may ride a skate board in the middle of the street. Even with warnings, he continues on as though nothing will happen. The ADHD child roughhouses with younger siblings, pets, or objects. He or she is oblivious to the fact that the behavior could be harmful or destructive. ADHD children seem to have no fear of strange people or possibly dangerous situations and act as if they are invincible.

Behavioral Excesses

As described previously, behavioral excesses are the continuation of activities when restraint or discontinuance would be more appropriate. These excesses can be categorized into the following four groups: (1) constant physical motion; (2) constant shifting of activity; (3) excessive talking; and (4) emotional excesses. Each of these categories will be discussed separately.

Constant Physical Motion

ADHD children cannot sit for more than a few minutes. They run and jump when they should be walking. For example, Sally constantly pokes or pushes other children whom she passes in the hallway at school. She may get up from her chair and wander around the classroom while other students are seated. Even when Sally is sitting, she constantly fidgets or plays with objects. Although she may be watching a TV show or video that interests her, Sally's body is still in motion. She cannot seem to make herself stop moving.

Constant Shifting of Activity

Constant shifting of activity is similar to what was discussed in the section on distractibility. The ADHD child is frequently distracted by sights and sounds that have nothing to do with the task at hand. For example, Curt can be working on arithmetic problems but the noise from a pencil dropped on the floor causes him to look around. His interest constantly moves from one object to another, resting for only a very brief second on each. The teacher is talking, but the various colors and shapes in the room or the movement of another student absorb his attention as much as what his teacher is saying. This constant shifting of activity occurs repeatedly throughout the day. Curt may be reading a book. However, a mark or tear on the page would be of as much concern as the words he is reading. He is overly attuned to the sensations of his body; even the rubbing of his clothes against his skin or minor itches become of major importance in competing for his overall attention.

Excessive Talking

The ADHD child typically talks more than other children in the group and continues to talk even when quiet is called for. For example, Margaret continues to talk repeatedly although a discussion has ended. The fact that others are not interested or annoyed with her makes no difference. She just talks louder or more rapidly to get their attention. Being called "motor mouth," or otherwise insulted or ignored, would deter most youngsters from continuing. However, this only seems to put fuel in the ADHD children's engine. They continue to push on without considering others.

Emotional Excesses

ADHD children have a low frustration tolerance. When confronted with adversity or challenge, it is not unusual for them to have a tantrum or become extremely excited. They may break toys, slam doors, or kick holes in a wall. If spanked, they become even more excitable, appearing to lose control. Unlike normal children, ADHD youngsters have great difficulty turning off their emotional motor. They become easily excited when playing active games with parents or peers. Although the other children can calm down when the activity has ended, ADHD children cannot stop. They continue to run, jump, poke, or push despite the fact they are becoming annoying. Even when others plead with the child to calm down, the ADHD youngster seems oblivious to their requests.

Determining the Causes of Hyperactivity

It is important to keep in mind that the ADHD child's behavioral symptoms manifest themselves consistently each day at home, in school, and in social situations. Although there may be variations of the behavior in different circumstances, the characteristics just described are common to all hyperactive youngsters. Thus, there is a good deal of similarity between ADHD children.

Despite the similarity of symptoms, the causes for the ADHD child's behavior can vary. In other words, there are a number of factors that can *cause* ADHD children to behave the way they do. For example, allergic reactions, diabetes, diseases, or actual damage to the brain can all be responsible for deviant and excessive activity in children. In addition, parental separation, divorce, or arguing and fighting in the child's presence can also cause a youngster to become frustrated, anxious, and depressed. The child's preoccupation with his or her emotional concerns stemming from parental discord can lead to distractibility and overactivity. Some children become overactive when they eat foods containing certain chemicals or additives. Exposure to certain dyes, perfumes, fragrances or other environmental irritants can also trigger excessive activity. Children reared in inadequate, chaotic, or disorganized homes might also suffer from ADHD. The parents have never taken the time and effort to train their youngsters to discipline and control themselves. Thus, when these children enter school, they lack the personal and social skills needed to be successful. They cannot concentrate or make themselves perform as expected because they never received the proper training.

The point to keep in mind is that there may be one or several causes responsible for the manifestation of those symptoms that indicate ADHD. In order to help the child, parents must try to identify each of these causes. It is not enough to simply diagnose the child as having ADHD and then assume that organic factors are responsible for the problem. Physicians often make this mistake and prescribe medication that, in many cases, only treats the symptoms. Unfortunately, such treatment is both incomplete and ineffective. It does not get to the root of the child's problems. Medication only deals with the symptoms and not the causes of ADHD. If parents are to develop effective treatment programs, a detailed history must be undertaken to identify those physical, cognitive, social, and emotional factors that are responsible for the child's maladaptive behavior. Once these factors are determined, then parents can develop a program to help the child to acquire the self-control, persistence, and the confidence to be successful.

Chapter 2

Medication: Why It Can Be Harmful

The Pressure to Medicate

In my professional experience, I have found the following to be typical of many parents whose children are diagnosed as ADHD and put on medication. First, the diagnosis of ADHD is usually made after the child begins school. Often the teacher is the person who initially complains about the youngster's behavior. The child's teacher tells the parents that he or she fails to complete assignments, stares into space, and is disruptive in the classroom. Parents are then told that medication is the answer to the child's problems. Since the ADHD youngster can't control him or herself, medication will help the child to sit quietly, pay attention, and improve learning. A recommendation is made to consult with the pediatrician as soon as possible. If the family doctor is reluctant to prescribe a drug, the school will then recommend a physician who is more cooperative. The school assumes that medication is the best solution and without it the child is destined to fail. Most parents have misgivings about medicating their child, but they realize the youngster will not learn if he or she does not become more manageable in the classroom. Thus, medication is an attractive alternative. It is presented as a quick fix to a difficult problem.

For obvious reasons, parents fear academic failure for their child. However, this is not the only factor influencing their decision to medicate. Trust in professionals often influences that decision as well. Parents want to trust those persons who are responsible for educating their child. They want to believe that physicians, teachers, and mental health specialists would only prescribe safe, effective treatment. As a result, parents often fail to ask about the existence and viability of other methods. They are told that medicine will calm the child and improve his or her concentration. They are further told that it will improve academic performance, even though there is evidence to the contrary. Given such limited information, parents often erroneously conclude that medication is both the best and only action to take.

Besides trust, the desire to be agreeable and cooperative also can influence the decision to medicate. Parents want to get along with their child's teacher. They are usually reluctant to challenge the school's opinion because they fear alienating themselves and their child. In fact, schools sometimes pressure parents to go along with their recommendations. They can insist that the distractible, disruptive child improve immediately. Suspensions, expulsions, or other punitive measures are sometimes threatened. Parents can sense when a teacher is becoming increasingly irritated with their ADHD child. This irritation may increase if they question the use of medication, which would make the teacher's job easier.

Further pressure is often applied when parents attend a team meeting. The team consists of all those professionals contributing to the child's education. It might include the teacher, the counselor, the school psychologist, a social worker, the school nurse, the principal, a special educator, or other school personnel. Each team member usually comments on the child's behavior. Evaluations and recommendations are presented while parents listen. Eventually they are asked to give their point of view regarding the team's analysis. Unfortunately, many parents are simply overwhelmed in this situation. They are unfamiliar both with educational procedures and jargon and don't know how to respond. It is extremely difficult for them to question or challenge the opinions of the "supposed" experts. Thus, many parents cooperate with the recommendation of medication. Facing a team of pro-medication professionals can be a very intimidating experience. If the family pediatrician also supports the use of drugs, based on teacher ratings and recommendations, this makes it even more difficult to resist. Parents usually become more convinced when the pediatrician is also pro-medication. With so many professionals supporting this position, it seems like the right choice. At this point, many parents repress their doubts. They agree to try the medication despite their uncertainties. It is easier to go along with the program and hope for the best.

In sum, many parents agree to a regimen of medication without fully understanding the consequences of their choice. In fact, parents are often unaware that other treatments are available. They have simply been advised that medication is the one and only solution to the child's problems. They do not know that counseling, diet, and behavior modification have all been successful in helping ADHD youngsters. Further, many parents have little or no knowledge of the possible hazards or long-term consequences of taking medication. Instead they believe the medicine will improve their child's academic performance and enhance his or her self-esteem. Again, there is little, if any, evidence to support this.[1,2]

Despite the continued strong support for medication, there are many parents who are now beginning to voice their concerns. Over the past year, there have been several news reports questioning the wisdom and efficiency of drug treatment for children. An article ("Behavior Pills: Disciplining Unruly Kids with a Potent Drug") in the 20 April 1987 issue of *Newsweek* reported that many children, who might need nothing more than counseling, were being treated with a drug called Ritalin. The article indicated that parents are becoming increasingly concerned about the dangers that Ritalin and other drugs might pose for their youngsters, both now and in the future. The concern of the parents is understandable. Medication *is* potentially harmful, physically and psychologically. The data indicate that medication does not improve academic performance; it does not build self-confidence; and it does not help a child to become responsible for his own behavior. In fact, I have treated many youngsters who have resisted taking the pill. They did not want to be different from their peers. They believed that taking pills made them "crazy" or "weird." They disliked the idea of taking a pill to control themselves. Most children want to be successful using their own cognitive and emotional resources. However, they are often confused as to how to cope with their difficulties. Unfortunately, the parents of ADHD children are equally bewildered. They are also unaware that there are better and safer ways to help their youngsters to achieve successfully.

Behavioral Drugs and Their Hazards

There are three medications typically used to treat ADHD children: Cylert, Ritalin, and Dexedrine. Parents who are interested in learning about these medications can consult the *Physician's Desk Reference,* which is published by Medical Economics Company Incorporated (Drandell, New Jersey 07649). Although this source is primarily for physicians, portions are written in non-medical language that parents can understand. The purpose of the *Physician's Desk Reference* is to make available essential information on prescription drugs. Thus, it can be a helpful source for understanding the benefits and liabilities of those medications prescribed for your child.

The *Physician's Desk Reference* specifically identifies a number of adverse reactions that can be caused by drugs prescribed for the treatment of ADHD. For example, adverse reactions for Cylert are identified for the liver, the blood, the central nervous system (the brain and spinal cord), the stomach, and intestine. The liver appears to be most effected by Cylert. Both hepatitis (inflammation of the liver) and jaundice (yellowness of the skin) have been reported. The PDR indicated there also have been isolated incidents of aplastic anemia, which occurs when the bone marrow fails in cell production. Other adverse reactions include convulsive seizures; Gilles de la Tourette syndrome (progressively violent muscular jerks of the face, shoulder, and extremities); hallucinations; dyskinetic (involuntary) movements of the tongue, lips, face, and extremities; mild depression; dizziness; increased irritability; headaches; insomnia (the most frequently reported side effect); nausea; stomach aches; and skin rash. It should be noted that the *Physician's Desk Reference* contains a warning that suppression of growth (decrements in predicted weight gain and/or height) has been reported with the long-term use of stimulants in children. Thus, the careful monitoring of patients requiring lengthy therapy is recommended.

Probably the most popular drug prescribed for ADHD children is Ritalin. However, like Cylert, there are a number of adverse reactions associated with its use. For example, loss of appetite, nervousness, abdominal pain, weight loss, insomnia, tachycardia (rapid heart beat), dizziness, dyskinetic movements, increases and decreases in blood pressure, and skin rash have been reported. As with Cylert, suppression of growth has been associated with the use of Ritalin and the close monitoring of patients requiring long-term therapy is recommended.

Dexedrine is the least popular of those drugs prescribed for treating ADHD youngsters. Many of the same adverse reactions described above occur with the use of this drug as well. To cite them again would simply be a repetition of the same old story. Hopefully, the point is clear. In order to calm your child through medication, you must be willing to expose him or her to potential hazards. Many of these reactions can be controlled by reducing the dosage or omitting the drug in the afternoon or evening. However, why expose a developing child to such risk? The answer to this question is particularly important in light of this statement from the *Physician's Desk Reference,* "Sufficient data on the safety and efficiency of long-term use [of these drugs with children] are not yet available." In other words, we cannot be sure that children placed on a drug regimen may not experience later medical problems. Cylert, Ritalin, and Dexedrine are not necessarily safe drugs. Again, is it worth the risk? Parents who put their children on medication often do so because they believe it will improve academic performance. The data indicate this is not true. Drugs may calm the child. However, they do not produce noticeable increases in academic skills or social adjustment. In fact, much of the evidence is to the contrary.[3,4]

The Psychological Pitfalls of Medication

Another problem frequently occurring with children diagnosed as ADHD is low self-esteem. Often they feel powerless and inferior as compared to their peers. In other words, ADHD children become depressed. They lack confidence in themselves. Putting a child on drugs only confirms that his or her behavior problems are caused by factors beyond their control. In fact, I recall one child calling Ritalin his "good boy pill." Another youngster referred to it as "my dope." What message are we conveying to a child when we place him or her on drugs? Aren't we telling the youngster that he or she is incapable of learning self-control and achieving success-fully on their own? Further, aren't we inadvertently increasing the likelihood that the child will fail to take responsibility for his or her behavior? Medication makes it easy to attribute success and failure to a pill. If the child does well, it is the pill that calmed the child and enabled him or her to concentrate. If the child fails, it's because he or she "forgot" or refused to take the medication. Most parents want to rear self-confident children. Parents want their children to plan ahead and to take responsibility for their own behavior. Keeping this in mind, it doesn't make sense to medicate children. It only confirms that we believe they lack the inner resources to control themselves and their environment. If a parent lacks confidence in a child, it is unlikely the child will believe in him or herself. A child looks to the parents for verification of his or her ability. If the parents become discouraged, we can expect the child to become discouraged as well. It is no wonder ADHD children often have such low self-esteem. Medication takes away the opportunity for them to prove that they, and not the pill, can be successful.

Medication doesn't make sense for another reason. There is research indicating that successful, achieving children develop what psychologists call an "internal locus of control."[5,6,7] This means these youngsters believe they are responsible for what happens to them. In other words, they believe their successes and failures are caused by their own behavior. Successful children avoid making excuses. It is not external events such as fate, luck, or other people that enable them to do well in life. Rather, it is their initiative that leads to success. Again, putting a child on medication is contrary to the notion of responsibility that parents want to instill in their children. Drug therapy suggests the child has a "disease." Medication arrests the disease, enabling the child to become calm and to concentrate better. The important point to remember is that drugs do not teach or train the child. Parents, teachers, and other adults are responsible for this. If we want responsible behavior and improved academic performance, it would be better to structure the environment to bring this about. Overactive youngsters can be trained to control themselves and to learn appropriate academic skills. In fact, there are several studies indicating that a high degree of environmental structure and consistent reinforcement produce such results. Thus, it makes more sense to work on behavioral control rather than simply to prescribe drugs as a cure-all to the problem.

There is another important point parents should consider before putting a child on a regimen of medication. The *Physician's Desk Reference* states that if drugs are prescribed for ADHD children, they should be used as "an integral part of a total treatment program which typically includes other remedial measures (psychological, educational, social) for a stabilizing effect." This means that medication should not be the only means for helping a child. Psychological, educational, and social methods should be used as well. In my experience, once a child is put on medication and it produces a calming effect, the drug becomes the total treatment program. Often the child does not receive special educational services despite the fact that he or she has a learning problem. Further, psychological and social problems are hardly ever addressed. It is assumed that if the child is more behaviorally compliant, the other problems will take care of themselves. However, this is hardly ever the case. Again, drugs do not teach academic skills or self-control. They do not teach the child to believe in him or herself or to cope effectively with problems.

Finally, it should be stressed that the *Physician's Desk Reference* states that medication is not indicated for all children with ADHD symptoms. Children who "exhibit symptoms secondary to environmental factors" should not be medicated. In other words, children whose over-activity is caused by environmental factors (such as broken or chaotic homes) should not be put on drugs. Rather, appropriate educational placement and psychological treatment is recommended. Many times children are medicated when, in actuality, environmental stress or lack of proper training are responsible for their over-activity and distractibility. Divorce, separation, and marital and family discord are becoming increasingly common in society. It's no wonder some children behave poorly. Medicating the child is not the cure for inadequate parenting or poor teaching. However, it often becomes the crutch for adults to lean on.

Chapter 3

Behavior Principles: Teaching Responsibility and Achievement

The Goals of Behavior Modification with Hyperactive Children

As indicated in the previous chapters, the research indicates that behavior modification, not drugs, has produced a significantly favorable effect on the academic performance of ADHD youngsters.[8, 9] Further, research has shown that successful children believe they succeed or fail because of the choices they make. This is called an "internal locus of control." Children who are generally successful tend to take responsibility for their behavior. They do not look to fate, luck, or other people to determine their success. Most parents want their children to be productive and achievement oriented. They want their children to think ahead, to make good choices, and to take responsibility for their actions. Although taking medication calms ADHD children, it teaches none of these skills. Medication does not train children to control themselves, to be persistent, or to plan ahead. Behavior modification, on the other hand, can be used to teach ADHD children to acquire these skills if it is properly applied.

One of the biggest complaints about ADHD children is that

they are impulsive. Impulsivity is acting without forethought or planning. Because ADHD children frequently fail to think or plan, they often do poorly in school and have interpersonal problems with adults and peers. Thus, ADHD children must learn to direct, control, and monitor their energy if they are to be successful. The behavioral program described in this chapter is designed to do this. It trains ADHD children to concentrate on a task, to delay gratification, and to think ahead. The program is designed so that children can learn that their behavior, and not external factors, is responsible for success and failure. I believe this is the most effective way of helping ADHD children to acquire the skills and confidence that is needed to be productive in life.

The Behavioral Principles of the Program

In order for an ADHD child, or any child, to learn to take responsibility, parents must begin by teaching the youngster that his or her behavior *causes* success or failure. The child must be taught two things: if he or she chooses to behave appropriately, positive consequences will follow; on the other hand, if he or she behaves inappropriately, negative consequences will follow. Parents usually begin to teach the latter when the child is very young. For example, Chuck is taught that if he puts his hand on a hot stove, he will get burned. It is important for Chuck to understand that putting his hand on the stove causes the pain to occur. In other words, his behavior, not the stove, is responsible for the burn. The message in this example is clear. Chuck is taught that if he thinks before acting, unnecessary pain can be avoided. Parents can use these common situations to point out the cause and effect relationship of human behavior. This instruction serves as a bulwark against impulsivity. It provides the basis for good planning and self-control.

There are a number of other everyday occurrences that can be used to teach the child to control his or her impulsivity and to plan ahead. For example, a common problem that a mother experiences is the child interrupting or making demands when she is talking on the telephone. The mother who attends to the interruption or gives in to the child's demands is actually rewarding this obnoxious behavior. Thus, the child is more likely to do this again and again.

In order to stop the behavior, the mother must state that interruptions and demands will not be tolerated. If they occur, the child will be sent to his or her room. Further, the child's request will not be granted. Mother must specifically point out to the child that interruptions and demands lead to punishment. They provide *no* chance of getting what one wants. Again, in this example, we are teaching the child to curb impulsivity and to anticipate consequences. This is the basis on which self-control is built.

Meals provide another opportunity for the parents to teach the child to plan ahead and to use good judgement. Consider the following: Emily gets up in the morning and orders "Crispy Crunchies" for breakfast. Mother pours the milk over the cereal. Fifteen minutes later Emily is dawdling and complaining that the cereal is soggy. She refuses to eat the cereal. A few hours later Emily begins to complain of hunger. Mother then makes her a pancake breakfast and she stops whining and complaining. What has Emily been taught? First, she has learned to avoid her responsibility for choosing the cereal for breakfast. Second, she has learned that if she cries and complains long and loud enough, mommy and/or daddy will take away the unpleasantness that she has brought on herself. Thus, in this simple everyday situation, the stage is set for teaching Emily poor frustration control, avoidance of responsibility, and poor planning skills. If parents continue to indulge their youngster in this manner over a number of years, it will lead to the development of a "spoiled child," who cannot tolerate even minimal adversity.

The purpose of these examples is to emphasize that there are a number of daily situations parents can use to teach children to be responsible, successful persons. However, in order to instruct them effectively, basic principles must be kept in mind. The following ten principles apply to children both with or without ADHD. Later in the chapter important principles will be discussed specifically for working with ADHD children. •

General Behavioral Principles for Rearing Successful Children

The following principles form the basis on which most behavior modification programs are built. The application of these is important in training children to develop good planning skills.

1. Practically all behavior, whether it is good or bad, is learned. Parents can teach their child to behave appropriately or inappropriately. This depends on how they respond to their child's actions.

2. Behavior that is followed by positive consequences is likely to continue. Behavior that is followed by negative consequences is likely to stop.

3. Research demonstrates that achievement-oriented children are often generously rewarded with affection and attention by their parents. Although money, toys, and food can follow good behavior and make it more likely that it will continue, children frequently seek praise. Thus, when parents follow good behavior with attention and praise as well as material rewards, they actually strengthen it. Parents, therefore, should actually look for good behavior and reward it with praise.

4. Children whose good behavior is recognized and rewarded by their parents, develop good feelings about themselves. Because their parents emphasize positive behaviors and are encouraging, they learn to expect to succeed. They learn that it is worth the time, effort, and commitment to try because success is always possible. Remember, this is the basis for the "internal locus of control," which was discussed previously.

5. Children will not continue to engage in desirable behavior simply because parents say it "ought" to be done or because parents tell them to do it. Desirable behavior continues because the consequences are positive. Undesirable behavior terminates because the consequences are negative. Parents therefore must apply the appropriate consequences to the right behavior. It is important not to inadvertently reward bad behavior or penalize or ignore good behavior.

6. If behavior is undesirable, there are two ways to eliminate it. We can ignore or punish it. Remember, behavior that is not followed with favorable consequences is likely to stop. If we cannot ignore a bad behavior, it may have to be punished. When punishment is used, it is important that the punishment fit the crime. For example, if Alex steals money from a parent, it would make no sense to hit him and restrict him from watching TV for six months. Rather, the logical consequence would be to have Alex repay the money or its equivalent in work time. In addition, Alex should

perform some extra work for the offended person. This is required because Alex not only stole from that person, but he inconvenienced him as well. Such a punishment is directly connected to the stealing offense. The parent who punishes in this manner is not engaging in overkill. Remember, excessive punishment leads to feelings of hopelessness and resentment in the child. Further, punishing a child with an "I-told-you-so" attitude only makes the youngster defensive. Such an atmosphere in the home is hardly conducive to teaching the child to develop an "internal locus of control." Rather, when a punishment is necessary, parents should indicate to the child that they are sorry that it must be administered—however, his or her behavior warranted it. This should be followed with encouragement to do better the next time.

7. Parental agreement on what constitutes desirable or undesirable behavior must be consistent and clearly communicated to the child. Disagreements between parents about expectations can cause confusion and negative feelings in the child. This is likely to lead to defensiveness and blaming instead of responsibility and achievement.

8. Remember, parents set examples for their children. Children learn by imitating those persons closest to them. If parents have a positive, achievement-oriented attitude, then this is likely to be transmitted to their children.

9. It takes time and effort to bring about behavioral change. If we want children to become responsible and achievement-oriented, this goal can only be achieved in a step-by-step fashion. Children should begin with small responsibilities like cleaning their room, taking out the trash, and so forth.

10. If parents want their child to understand the kind of behavior that they expect, they must be concrete in describing it. Thus, instead of saying "be nice," "be good," "be pleasant," parents should make statements such as, "eat all of the spinach on your plate," "put your plate in the sink," or "be dressed for bed by 9:00 p.m."

In summary, it is important to keep the following in mind. First, there are situations occurring each day that parents can use to teach their child to plan ahead and to use good judgment. It is up to the parents to take advantage of these opportunities. Second, parents must remember that what follows a behavior determines whether or not it will continue . Thus, they should always give the reward *after* the demonstration of responsibility, not before. For example, when parents want their child to eat vegetables, they should make a statement such as, "First eat the peas and then you can have the ice cream." Most people recognize that if the child is allowed to eat the ice cream first, the peas will only be eaten later and after much effort. This is generally true for all activities that require hard work and effort. If the reward is given first, procrastination is likely to follow. This occurs because the motivation to work has been taken away. Common sense tells us that. For example, how often does a child complete homework satisfactorily if the youngster starts it after watching TV or playing all day?

Behavioral Principles Specifically for the ADHD Child

The ADHD child has marked difficulty with concentration and impulsivity. The following suggestions should be considered in the implementation of any behavior modification program.

1. Because the ADHD child has difficulty with concentration, often the youngster does not remember what he or she has been asked to do. This occurs even though directions or instructions might have been given a short time earlier. In order to help the child to remember, parents should ask the child to restate the given information. If the youngster is able to do this, he or she should be praised or rewarded. If the child's recall is poor, however, the directions should be given again until he or she can accurately give them back. When giving instructions, the parents should make sure the child is making eye contact with them. It is important that the child's behavior shows that he or she is listening. This makes it more likely that the child will remember the directions the first time. In some cases it is helpful to have the child actually practice or demonstrate the required behavior in the parent's presence. This can further deepen the child's understanding of what is expected.

2. Each evening parents should have a meeting with their child. They should discuss the activities that the child has per-

formed successfully and unsuccessfully for that day. At the end of the meeting, the child should be asked to summarize these. This indicates to the parents that he or she is listening and understands what they are saying. If the child makes mistakes or omits information in the summary, parents should make the necessary corrections. The child is then asked to review the behaviors again. It is important to remember that repetition will enhance the ADHD child's concentration and memory. This makes it more likely the child will retain the information conveyed to him or her.

3. The ADHD child responds best to a consistent environment. Thus, the same behaviors should be required in sequence each day with little or no variation. This helps the child to get into a routine. In constructing a consistent environment, it is important to specify times, places, and participants. When old behaviors become a habit, then new ones can be required or added to the program.

4. The hyperactive child becomes frustrated easily. Thus, it is important to reward the youngster frequently when he demonstrates good self-control. When the child is disappointed or is having difficulty but *does not* lose his or her temper, parents should comment on this. Specifically, the child should be told that he or she is showing good self-control. Parents praise of self-control is rewarding to the ADHD child.

5. The ADHD child is easily excited. He or she has much difficulty remaining calm and controlling emotions. Thus, it is important for parents to be low-key. Since the ADHD child loses control easily, parents must try to remain calm themselves. Avoid condemnations such as, "You're a bad boy (or girl)," or "You're so dumb." If the child is behaving badly, parents should try to stop the behavior *early* before it gets out of hand. They should specifically comment on the behavior and request that it come under immediate control. If this does not work, the child should be removed to another room or an isolated location until he or she becomes calm again.

6. The ADHD child loses his or her temper quickly. Teaching the youngster how to maintain control is a helpful strategy. When the child begins to feel frustrated, he or she can be instructed to take a deep breath and count to ten. The youngster can then repeat the words, "be calm." When the youngster regains control, he or

she can talk with the parents about the problem. They can then suggest appropriate ways to cope with frustration.

7. Because the ADHD child has such difficulty with concentration and self-control, inventing exercises to practice these can be helpful. For example, parents can make up games such as having the child sit in a chair without moving his or her hands, legs, or head for a specified period of time. Or the child might be asked to carry out silly commands like, "take a book from the shelf with your left hand and kneel on it with your right knee." Such exercises train the child in both body control and listening. Successful completion of these exercises should be praised or rewarded.

8. The ADHD child can divide the parents and cause difficulty in the marriage. Thus, it is important for *both* parents to agree on the expected behaviors and methods for rewarding and penalizing the child. Sometimes if one parent believes the other is "too hard," then he or she will try to compensate by being "easy." This does not work. It will cause arguments, sometimes right in the child's presence. Parents must support each other and strive for consistency.

9. The parent who is primarily responsible for rearing a hyperactive child will need to be relieved from the "combat zone" from time to time. Otherwise discouragement and "battle fatigue" will set in. It is important for the primary caretaker to pursue some form of relaxation for the purpose of rejuvenating. Thus, babysitters, supportive grandparents, friends, or the other parent must be asked to take the child from time to time.

10. In setting up a behavior modification program, it is important to begin with tasks that the child can accomplish relatively easily. The ADHD child often becomes easily discouraged. This occurs because the youngster has little confidence in his or her ability to be successful. By starting with relatively easy tasks, the child can see immediate progress. This will encourage him or her to continue trying. Once the child has been repeatedly successful, then more difficult tasks can be requested. He or she will now have the confidence to attempt new challenges.

11. The ADHD child is very distractible. Therefore, when trying to get his or her attention, it is important to minimize or eliminate competing stimuli in the environment. In other words,

don't have TV, radio, or other distracting sights or sounds around that can distract the child. Keep the youngster focused on what he or she is required to do.

In summary, the ADHD child has special problems that must be kept in mind. He or she is distractible, inattentive, and impulsive. These characteristics must be taken into account in planning a behavioral program. Because the ADHD child is so distractible, it is important that parents require the child to attend to what they are saying. They must make sure that the youngster makes eye contact and behaves as though he or she were listening to them. Having the child repeat instructions helps the child to retain information. It also enables the parents to be sure the youngster understands what they expect.

One of the biggest problems for the ADHD child is impulsivity. Parents can train the child to be less impulsive and to show greater self-control if they actively praise or reward it. In addition, parents can teach the child to think before he or she acts by using simple games and exercises.

Finally, parental consistency is very important in dealing with the ADHD child. Parents must agree on expected behaviors and appropriate rewards and penalties. They must remain low key because the ADHD child becomes easily excited. Further, the ADHD child often gets discouraged and gives up easily. He or she lacks self-confidence. Thus, it is important for parents to be encouraging and to provide experiences that will enable the child to achieve successfully. This will help the youngster to believe in his or her ability to overcome challenges and adversities.

The Behavior Modification Program

In the preceding discussion we dealt with how the ADHD child is both distractible and impulsive. Examples were provided of how the child often does not plan ahead and fails to sustain concentrated, goal-oriented effort. The program that follows is designed to overcome these problems. It is based on the assumption that if parents want their child to be responsible and achievement-oriented, they must follow these behaviors with pleasant consequences. By rewarding good planning and sustained effort, the ADHD child's problems with distractibility and impulsivity can be better controlled. In fact, the program is designed to train the ADHD child to make productive use of his or her high level of energy.

This program uses material rewards to motivate the child to complete work-oriented tasks. However, the material rewards are used to merely "prime the pump," so to speak. Such rewards motivate the child to perform unpleasant tasks that in the long run will help to develop good work habits. If the ADHD youngster learns to consistently fulfill responsibilities, it makes it more likely he or she will acquire the feeling of satisfaction for a job well-done. As these feelings of satisfaction occur repeatedly, the successful completion of work-related tasks will more than likely become their own reward. Thus, the motivation to initiate and sustain concentrated effort to achieve goals becomes "internally" rather than "externally" controlled. The material rewards will then no longer be necessary. The child will now have learned how to motivate him or herself.

One other point should be considered in the following program. Although many parents may be familiar with behavior modification procedures, this program is designed with a specific purpose in mind. The purpose is to train the ADHD child to not only engage in responsible behaviors, but to sustain them over an extended period of time. Thus, the program is geared to teach the child to organize and plan ahead on a daily, weekly, and even a monthly basis. It actually trains the child to defer immediate gratification and to exercise self-control and good judgment. In fact, the child can only be successful in the program by developing skills in these areas. For example, if the child does not plan ahead and organize properly, he or she will not complete responsibilities within the appropriate time limits. This will result in the loss of special treats and privileges that most youngsters find desirable. On the other hand, if the child organizes and plans appropriately, valuable short- and long-term rewards can be earned. Thus, through this approach, the child can learn that thinking ahead and the willingness to work can lead to the achievement of worthwhile goals.

With the preceding information in mind, the next step is to specifically design the behavioral program. The first program that will be presented is effective with youngsters from approximately four to twelve years of age. A program for children between the ages of two and four will be discussed at the conclusion of this chapter. In setting up the program, it is important to first decide on the specific behaviors the child is to perform each day. Next, the behaviors must be listed in chronological order beginning with (in order of their occurrence) the morning behaviors, followed by the afternoon behaviors, and lastly, the evening behaviors.

Some behaviors that might be on the list include:

Morning behaviors	*Afternoon behaviors*	*Evening behaviors*
1. Be completely dressed by 7:30 a.m.	1. Eat all lunch without complaining.	1. Eat supper without complaining.
2. Wash hands and face.	2. Put clothes away.	2. Wash dishes.
3. Comb hair.	3. Homework done neatly and accurately.	3. Take bath.
4. Eat all breakfast without complaining.	4. Put school materials in bookbag for next day.	4. Brush teeth
5. Brush teeth.	5. Put toys away.	5. Ready for bed by 8:30 p.m.

In determining behaviors, it is important to list some tasks that the child is likely to complete relatively easily as well as some difficult ones. This will enhance the likelihood that the ADHD youngster will receive positive feedback for being successful. Further, it will motivate the youngster to try more difficult tasks that will also be required.

Once the behaviors have been determined and arranged in chronological sequence, they can be organized on a chart so the child can follow them through the day. (See chart, page 30.)

For children who cannot read, parents can draw pictures of the required activity or use pictures cut out from magazines. These serve as visual cues to remind the child about the task. Also, the chart can have a title like "Big Boy (or Big Girl) Chart." This lets the youngster know that successful performance demonstrates responsibility and maturity. For older children, titles such as "Maturity (or Responsibility) Chart" might be used.

Once this has been completed, the next step is to identify

Big Boy (or Girl) Behavior Chart

	Sun	Mon	Tues	Wed	Thurs	Fri	Sat	Weekly Totals
Morning								
1. Dressed by 7:30 a.m.								
2. Properly groomed								
3. Eat breakfast w/o complaining								
Afternoon								
1. Homework done								
2. Take out trash								
3. Clean room								
Evening								
1. Eat supper w/o complaining								
2. Take bath								
3. Brush teeth								
4. Ready for bed by 8:30 p.m.								

inappropriate behaviors. These can be called "Baby Behaviors" because they show immaturity and a lack of responsibility. Again, titles like "Immature (or Irresponsible) Behaviors" can be used with older children. These would be set up on the following chart:

Baby behaviors	Sun	Mon	Tues	Wed	Thurs	Fri	Sat	Weekly Totals
1. Cussing								
2. Tantrum								
3. Lying								
4. Stealing								
5. Disobedience								
6. Back talk								

A list of inappropriate behaviors is included because it provides the child with feedback about actions that show poor self-control. However, it is important to emphasize the positive behaviors. These bring praise from parents and others. It is this praise and encouragement that ultimately teaches the ADHD child that he or she is capable of self-control and achievement.

With the completion of the behavior chart, the next step is to develop a list of rewards that can be earned by successful performance of the tasks. These rewards should be special treats that ordinarily could not be obtained during the course of the day, week, or month. For example, special daily treats might include staying up an extra half-hour in the evening or ordering a special dessert or snack. A special weekly treat requires the child to behave responsibly for a longer period. Thus, a bigger prize is offered such as going to a restaurant or a movie. A super special treat would require responsible behavior for two, three, or four weeks. Such treats might consist of a trip to an amusement park, both a movie and a restaurant, or earning an expensive toy. Three separate lists on one chart enables the child to see what can be earned daily, weekly, and over the long-term:

Daily Special Treats	*Weekly Special Treats*	*Super Special Treats*
1. 1 hr. T.V. special	1. Fast food restaurant $1.50 limit	1. Amusement park (4 weeks—95%)
2. ½ hr. extra staying up past bedtime	2. Movie	2. Camping (4 weeks—95%)
3. Special dessert	3. Skating	3. Restaurant of choice (4 weeks—90%)
4. Gum (1 piece)	4. Friend over for night	4. Trip to arcade $5 limit (3 wks.—80%)
5. Soft drink	5. Friend for dinner	5. Fishing (3 weeks—80%)
6. Ice cream	6. Popcorn party	6. Baseball game (4 weeks—90%)
7. Chips	7. Order favorite meal at home	7. $5 toy (4 weeks—80%)
8. ½ hr. play game with parent	8. Stay up 2 hrs. over bedtime—limit 1 night on weekend	8. $10 toy (4 weeks—90%)
9. Popcorn	9. $2 toy	9. Movie with friend, parent pay (2 weeks—90%)
10. Candy snack	10. Pizza	10. Bowling w/friend, parent pay (3 weeks—90%)

The behavior and reward charts might look like the following example. (See chart, pages 33–34.) Note that the behavior chart tells the child what is expected and the reward chart tells what can be earned.

The reader will note that the behavior chart contains a percentage column. This portion tells the child how well he or she has done for the day and the week. The percentage determines whether the child will receive a reward. When the day is complete, the parent should compute the percentage and write it in the space provided. The child at this time can receive the reward. Depending on the reward, it may have to be delivered the following day.

The reward system is based on the following guidelines. If the child completes 80 percent of the responsibilities with no baby behaviors, he or she would get to choose one item from the daily special treats column for that day. For 90 percent with no baby behaviors, two treats could be given. For a perfect day, three treats could be obtained. If the youngster engages in a baby behavior, the successful performance of one responsibility is cancelled out. For example, let's suppose the child was ready for school on time, but then lied about something later. Lying would cancel out the credit he or she would have received for being ready on time. Thus, the overall percentage for the day would be lowered.

The weekly special treats would be delivered the same as the daily specials. If the child completed 80 percent of all possible responsible behaviors, he or she could choose one weekly special treat from the reward list. For 90 percent, two weekly specials could be obtained. For a perfect week, three treats could be purchased. Remember that the daily treats should be small prizes, whereas the weekly prizes should be worth more. It is important for the parents to deliver the rewards when the child has earned them. They should not promise something they cannot deliver. This will discourage the child and decrease the motivation to perform.

The super special treat list differs from the daily and weekly specials because the delivery of these rewards is more expensive, more time-consuming and, more demanding of the parent's energy. Since these rewards are much more valuable, the child must behave

BIG BOY (OR GIRL) CHART								
	Sun	Mon	Tues	Wed	Thurs	Fri	Sat	Weekly %
Morning 1. Dressed by 7:30 a.m.								
2. Eat breakfast w/o complaints								
3. Brush teeth								
Afternoon 1. Homework done								
2. Pick up toys								
3. Feed dog								
Evening 1. Eat supper w/o complaints								
2. Wash dishes								
3. Take bath								
4. Ready for bed by 8:30 p.m.								
PERCENTAGES								
Baby behaviors 1. Complaining								
2. Tantrum								
3. Swearing								
4. Disobedience								
5. Taking things w/o permission								
6. Lying								
PERCENTAGES								

Daily Special Treats	*Weekly Special Treats*	*Super Special Treats*
1. Gum (1 piece)	1. Movie	1. Baseball game (4 weeks—80%)
2. Soft drink	2. Bowling	2. Fishing (2 weeks—80%)
3. Ice cream	3. Friend overnight	3. Amusement Park (4 weeks—95%)
4. Candy snack	4. Go to friend's overnight	4. $7 toy (3 weeks—90%)
5. Stay up extra ½ hr.	5. Pizza	5. Videogame cartridge (4 wks.—90%)
6. Play game w/parent ½ hr.	6. Fast food restaurant $1.50 limit	6. Camping (3 weeks—95%)

responsibly for two, three, or four weeks to obtain them. The purpose of this list is to reward the child for working for extended periods of time in order to obtain more worthwhile goals. Further, in order to earn these items, the child must plan ahead. It should be noted that on the sample super special treats list, the time and percentage needed to obtain the long-term rewards varies. For example, the youngster would need an 80 percent performance for two weeks to go fishing. However, a trip to the amusement park, which might be more expensive and time-consuming, requires a 95 percent performance for four weeks. By arranging the rewards on a two, three, and four week delivery basis with increasing percentages, parents are actually shaping the child to sustain good work habits over longer periods of time. In this way the child can learn that persistent effort can lead to the achievement of more worthwhile goals in the future. Again, as with the daily and weekly rewards, parents must be willing to invest the time, expense, and energy to ensure the delivery of super special treats when they are earned. If parents promise a super special treat, they must be prepared to follow through if the program is to have credibility.

Once the chart is completed, the program is ready to be implemented. Each time a behavior is performed satisfactorily, a visible sign such as a gold star, a "smilie face," or even a check is placed in the box beside the behavior for that day. Preferably, this is done immediately after the activity is completed. In the initial stages of the program, the ADHD child might need a reminder before performing an activity. More than one reminder is unacceptable, however, and the child should not receive a sticker. Further, after a few weeks, no reminders should be given since parents want the child to learn to function independently. It is important that parental nagging not become the catalyst for bringing about good behavior. Rather, it must come from the child. This will teach the child to be responsible for him or herself. One other point should be kept in mind when the child completes a task satisfactorily. Parents should say to the child, "I like the way you made your bed and cleaned your room" or "you did a good job washing the dishes." In other words, parents should tell the child that his or her behavior pleased them.

If the child behaves badly, negative feedback must also be provided. A visible sign such as a "frownie face" or a minus sign can be used. Again, specific feedback about the behavior must be provided such as the following statement: "When you dawdle while dressing in the morning, it causes you to be late for breakfast. Please dress more quickly the next time." This statement tells the child what he or she did wrong and why this behavior was harmful. Also, the statement provides the child with a better alternative. When parents reprimand, they may find that their child will get upset or defensive, and he or she may not listen to their explanations. If this occurs, it is best to remove the youngster from the situation until he or she is calm and ready to listen. Remember, arguing or "logicing" with a distraught child will seldom, if ever, be successful. Adult reasons and emotional controls develop over a lifetime. However, the ADHD child has only limited insight as well as more difficulty keeping emotions under control.

Another helpful suggestion in implementing this program is to have the ADHD child read the expected behaviors. Then have the youngster repeat them without looking at the chart. The youngster should be praised for each behavior he or she remembers and reminded of those he or she forgets. If the child cannot read, parents should have the youngster explain the pictures. Then they can have the youngster explain the behaviors without looking at the pictures. Remember, having the ADHD child verbally repeat the behaviors makes it more likely he or she will retain them and behave appropriately.

Another strategy is also useful in teaching the ADHD child to think ahead and to avoid the temptation of evading responsibility. The youngster and the parents can select special shows from a schedule of TV programs that the child would like to see when his or her work is completed. Further, the youngster might pick out some of the weekly and super special treats he or she would like to obtain. This approach teaches the child to plan so that he or she can achieve goals more readily.

An example of a completed chart and an interpretation of how it would be used with an actual child is provided on page 37.

Note that on the first day (Sunday), the child scored 100%. Therefore, the youngster would get to choose three daily special treats from the reward chart presented below.

Daily Special Treats
1. Candy snack
2. 1 hr. T.V. special
3. ½ hr. extra on bedtime
4. Special dessert
5. Pizza slice
6. 1 piece gum
7. Soft drink
8. Ice cream
9. Chips or popcorn
10. Play game w/parent ½ hour

On Monday, although the youngster completed nine of the ten responsibilities satisfactorily, one bad behavior occurred. This dropped the daily percentage to 80 instead of 90 because the one "frownie face" cancelled out one of the "smilie faces." Therefore, only one special treat could be obtained for that day. On Saturday, all of the responsibilities were completed satisfactorily. However, there were three violations. Thus, three responsibilities were cancelled out. Since the child's daily percentage was only 70, no daily special treats could be obtained. The reader will note that weekly as well as daily percentages are given for each task. Also, a total percentage for the week is provided, which in this case is 89. Thus, the child can obtain one weekly special treat from the reward chart presented on page 38.

BIG BOY (OR GIRL) CHART								
	Sun	Mon	Tues	Wed	Thurs	Fri	Sat	Weekly Totals
Morning 1. Ready for school by 7:30 a.m.	☺		☺	☺	☺	☺	☺	6/7 86%
2. Eat breakfast w/o complaining	☺	☺	☺	☺	☺	☺	☺	7/7 100%
3. Brush teeth	☺	☺	☺	☺	☺	☺	☺	7/7 100%
Afternoon 1. Complete homework	☺	☺	☺	☺	☺	☺	☺	7/7 100%
2. Put toys away	☺	☺	☺	☺	☺	☺	☺	7/7 100%
3. Take out trash	☺	☺	☺	☺	☺	☺	☺	7/7 100%
Evening 1. Set table	☺	☺	☺	☺		☺	☺	6/7 86%
2. Take bath	☺	☺	☺	☺	☺	☺	☺	7/7 100%
3. Brush teeth	☺	☺	☺	☺	☺	☺	☺	7/7 100%
4. Ready for bed by 8:30 p.m.	☺	☺	☺	☺	☺	☺	☺	7/7 100%
Baby Behaviors 1. Complaining		☹					☹	2
2. Tantrum					☹		☹	2
3. Swearing					☹			1
4. Disobedience			☹					1
5. Taking things w/o permission								
6. Lying							☹	1
PERCENTAGES	100%	80%	90%	100%	80%	100%	70%	89%

Weekly Special Treats
1. Trip to fast food restaurant $1.50 limit
2. Movie
3. Skating
4. Friend overnight
5. Friend for lunch
6. Stay overnight w/friend
7. $2 toy
8. Popcorn party w/friend
9. Order favorite meal at home
10. Stay up 1½ hours beyond bedtime on weekend

Although this case example covers only through the weekly special treats chart, the same principles that were previously discussed would be applied in obtaining super special treats. The only difference is the child would have to behave responsibly for a longer period of time. Note that on the super special treats chart, a time period and percentage of successfully completed tasks is indicated. This enables the youngster to know in advance what is required to obtain the reward.

Super Special Treats
1. Restaurant (2 weeks—90%)
2. Amusement park (4 weeks—95%)
3. Camping (3 weeks—95%)
4. Fishing (4 weeks—90%)
5. Baseball game (4 weeks—90%)
6. $5 toy (4 weeks—90%)
7. Movie w/friend parents pay (3 weeks—90%)
8. Arcade $2.50 limit (2 weeks—80%)
9. Fast food restaurant w/friend $4 limit (2 weeks—90%)
10. Trip to zoo (3 weeks—80%)

While administering this program, it is helpful to have a family meeting for about ten or fifteen minutes each evening. At this time parents can go over the good and bad behaviors of the day with the child. Again, it is important to emphasize the successful completion of positive behaviors. However, there are behaviors parents will want their child to work on. These must be brought to the youngster's attention so he can improve his or her performance. At the end of the meeting, the parents should ask the child to name those behaviors that were done well. Also, the child should identify what he or she needs to work on the next day. If the youngster can state the behaviors accurately, he or she should be praised. If the child forgets some points, the parent should help the youngster to identify what he or she forgot. By using this approach, the parents will be teaching their youngster to concentrate on what they are saying. This is essential to learning and improving one's performance.

As indicated previously, this program will be effective with children from approximately four to twelve years of age. In order to work with youngsters from two to four years of age, a more simplified version is required. Thus, the following suggestions are offered. With two- to four-year-olds, parents should demonstrate and explain the appropriate behaviors. Further, they should be sure to have the child actually perform them as well. When the child engages in a "big boy" or "big girl" behavior, praise should be given immediately, as well as some tangible reward. For example, the parents can set up a game with the child called SPACE SHIP TO THE MOON. This can be drawn such as the following illustration:

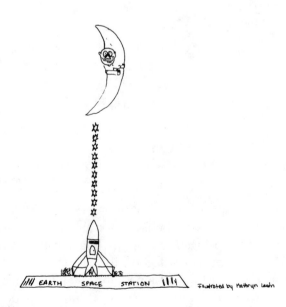

Each time the child exhibits an appropriate behavior, the space ship would move forward one space. For an inappropriate behavior, it would go backward one space. When the space ship arrives at the moon, a special treat such as a candy bar, chips, or some other inexpensive reward could be given. For long-term rewards of higher value, the planets might also be included on the chart with ten spaces between each planet. When the child completes the journey and arrives back to the earth space station, a special treat may be given. Smaller treats can be provided when landing at each of the individual planets along the way. A similar approach to this might be as follows: Draw or cut out pictures of small treats (such as candy, chips, or small trinkets) and special treats (such as a stuffed animal, a baseball game, or a movie advertisement) and paste them on a chart with ten spaces between each treat. A picture of a boy or girl or an actual photograph of the child can be placed at the starting point. This would be moved forward or backward depending on whether the child behaved appropriately or inappropriately. An example of such a chart is presented below:

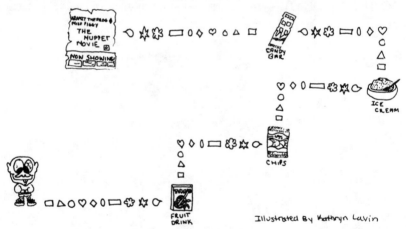

Illustrated By Kathryn Lavin

Note that the special treat (a movie) comes only after the child has engaged in responsible behavior for an extended time period. Parents should keep in mind that any board game (for example, Candyland Bingo) provides a good format on which a child can move forward or backward, depending on his or her behavior. Remember, when the child arrives at an important point on the chart, small or big treats can be given based on how long and how hard the child has worked.

Another technique, which is helpful with younger children, is to take a picture of a toy and cut it into a number of parts. The individual parts can be put together like a puzzle. Each time the youngster performs successfully, one of the parts can be assembled. If the child behaves inappropriately, one part is taken away. When the entire puzzle is completed, the youngster can then go with the parents to purchase the toy.

Another very simple approach that can be used with small children is to buy a variety of stickers (such as Snoopy or other cartoon and animal characters) and gold or other multi-colored stars. Take a large piece of paper and draw a picture of a "smilie face" with "Good Boy" (or Girl) printed on the top. Each time the child behaves responsibly, he or she can choose a sticker and paste it on the paper. A special sticker, such as Snoopy or some other favorite, can be awarded when a particularly difficult task that requires extra self-control is mastered. For example, when the child works at tying his or her shoes without fussing, a special sticker might be given.

In conclusion, in working with children between the ages of two and four, it is important that parents have the child both verbally repeat and demonstrate behaviorally what is expected. Further, the parents must praise the child after each behavior and provide immediate feedback using one of the techniques discussed previously. This shows the child that the parents are interested in successful performance. By reinforcing appropriate behavior, parents are helping to build achievement-oriented attitudes for the future. One final point should be stressed. The use of material rewards and charts is a simple technique to motivate the child to plan ahead, to use good judgment, and to persist in the achievement of worthwhile goals. This approach is utilized because it provides the ADHD child with the structure and incentive to want to do well. As the child *learns* to organize his or her time properly and develops good work habits, these external cues and motivators will become less necessary. In fact, when the child learns to perform responsibilities thoroughly and consistently, they will not be needed at all. At this point the pursuit of excellence and the satisfaction of a job well done becomes its own reward. It is this attitude that parents want to foster in their child. Behavior modification is simply one of the tools that can help achieve this goal.

Chapter 4

Diet Control: The Elimination of Environmental Irritants

Background

Nearly twenty-five years ago, a pediatrician named Benjamin Feingold began to show that certain foods and additives had a negative effect on some children's behavior. His experiences were described in two books titled *Why Your Child Is Hyperactive* and *The Feingold Cookbook*. According to Dr. Feingold, over half of the hyperactive children placed on his dietary program showed a significant improvement in their behavior. Dr. Feingold shared his results with both professionals and the public. He asked the scientific community to conduct further research to determine how different foods and their ingredients affect us. Dr. Feingold also encouraged the formation of support groups. The purpose of support groups was twofold. First, they were to generate public awareness about the importance of eliminating certain foods and synthetic additives from the diet in the treatment of behavior, learning, and health problems. Second, the members were to provide help to each other in implementing the Feingold Dietary Program. Through Dr. Feingold's leadership, The Feingold Association of the United States (Box 6550, Alexandria, VA 22306) was formed. It now serves as the hub for the various local branches that exist throughout the country. These local associations disseminate information and initiate programs in order to educate people on the importance of nutritional management in the control of behavior.

The Feingold Program of Diet Management

As indicated above, the Feingold program requires that certain foods and additives be removed from the diet of ADHD children because these foods have been associated with behavior, learning, and health problems. The Feingold program is implemented in two stages.[10] In stage one, two groups of food are eliminated. First, all foods that contain synthetic or artificial colors and flavors must be removed from the diet. Synthetic colors are sometimes listed on labels as "U.S. Certified Colors" or by a Food and Drug Administration number, such as "FD & C Yellow No. 5." Synthetic flavors, on the other hand, may be referred to as "flavoring" or "artificial flavoring." Besides eliminating artificial colors and flavors, three anti-oxidant preservatives must be removed as well. These are listed as, BHA (Butylated Hydroxyanisole), BHT (Butylated Hydroxyluene) and TBHQ (Monotertiary Butyehydroxylquinone).

Identifying the colors, flavors, and preservatives in processed food begins by reading the manufacturer's label. For example, the manufacturer of a strawberry ice cream bar listed the ingredients as follows: fresh milk, nonfat milk, cream, sugar, corn syrup, stabilizer (Cellulose Gel and Gum, Mono and Diglycerides, Salt, Polysorbate 80, Carrgeenan), vanilla extract, water, annatto color, strawberries, pectin, natural flavor, citric acid, modified food starch, locus bean gum, and artificial color. This product could not be included in the ADHD child's diet because it lists "artificial color," which makes it an unacceptable food in the Feingold program.

After removing artificial colors, flavors, and preservatives from the diet, temporarily eliminating those foods containing natural salicylates (the acid substances giving fruits their tangy taste) must be undertaken. Listed alphabetically these foods include: almonds, apples (also cider and cider vinegar), apricots, bananas, berries, cherries, cloves, coffee, cucumbers (including pickles), currants, grapes (also raisins, wine, and wine vinegar), green peppers (also chilies), nectarines, oil of wintergreen (methyl salicylate), oranges, peaches, pineapples, plums, prunes, tangerines, tea, and tomatoes.

The elimination of artificial colors, flavors, preservatives, and natural salicylates from the diet should lead to improved behavior in ADHD children within one to six weeks. Generally, younger children seem to progress more rapidly then older youngsters. Once behavior improves, it should be allowed to stabilize for about four to six weeks. Foods containing natural salicylates can gradually be returned to the child's diet. The purpose of the gradual return of these foods is to determine those foods containing natural salicylates that can and cannot be tolerated. This enables parents to expand and restrict the diet accordingly. In making this determination, it is important to keep a diary indicating what food has been eaten and any changes observed in behavior, sleep patterns, and school and work performance. Recording this information makes it more likely to identify those foods causing a behavior problem. The Feingold Association recommends the following steps be taken in reintroducing salicylates into the child's diet:

1. Introduce only one salicylate at a time. Use the new food several times for about a week unless deterioration in behavior occurs. Note any behavior changes in a diary.
2. If possible, use fresh, unprocessed locally grown salicylate fruits and vegetables that are in season.
3. If there are no negative reactions to the first salicylate, wait several days and introduce another one.

It is possible the child may react negatively to the first salicylate reintroduced to the diet. However, this does not mean that other salicylates can't be tolerated. Should an adverse reaction occur, wait about a week, and then introduce another salicylate. It is important to remember that children may react differently to the *form* of the different salicylates in their diet. For example, a youngster may not be able to tolerate a dried fruit. However, when that same fruit is eaten in a cooked or raw form, the same child is able to tolerate it. Interestingly, some children can cope with a salicylate when it is cooked, dried, or raw. However, when the fruit is more highly condensed in the form of juices, jellies, or syrup, these youngsters may react negatively. Such response variability makes it even more imperative that a careful record be kept of the *type, quantity,* and the *form* of the food that is eaten. Without careful, exact notations, pinpointing those foods that cannot be tolerated becomes increasingly difficult.

One final point must be considered in implementing the Feingold program: the elimination of aspirin and medication containing aspirin. Aspirin has also been associated with behavior and learning problems in some children, and therefore should be eliminated. Again, parents must be sure to read the labels of any medication that the child is taking, which may contain aspirin.

Troubleshooting if Diet Management Isn't Working

As mentioned previously, following the Feingold program usually leads to a behavioral improvement in one to six weeks. If this does not occur, there may be some identifiable causes:[11]

1. Failure to stay on the diet.
2. Excessive use of sugar.
3. The failure to eliminate all salicylates from the diet.
4. Using similar products but not the same as the Feingold list of approved foods, which can be obtained from a local branch of the Feingold Association.
5. Using a brand of shampoo, toothpaste, soap, vitamins, or medication containing artificial colors or flavors.

Parents must attempt to identify the potential culprits if the diet does not appear to be working. Further, parents need to examine other possible chemicals and foods that might be responsible for the child's failure to improve. The old addage, "one man's meat is another man's poison" certainly applies in implementing the Feingold program successfully. For example, one child might tolerate a certain *quantity* and *form* of sugar quite well. However, this same quantity and form of sugar might cause another child to behave poorly. In fact, Dr. Feingold commented on the relationship of sugar to hyperactivity. He indicated that not only cane sugar, but all simple sugars (brown and beet sugars, corn syrup, molasses, and honey) can negatively affect behavior. It has been reported that some children react negatively to chocolate, milk, pork, wheat, corn, and eggs. Food additives such as monosodium glutamate (MSG; used as a flavor enhancer for meats, gravies, soups, sauces, and Chinese food), calcium propionate (a preservative used in bread), sodium benzoate (synthetic preservative) and corn syrup (sweetener produced by treating cornstarch with chemicals) can trigger behavioral disturbances.

Besides foods and additives, irritants such as synthetic scents, colors, and flavors in non-food products can also cause negative reactions. Some examples include:

1. Household products such as furniture polishes, floor waxes, rug sprays, and scented air fresheners.
2. Laundry products such as detergents and scented fabric softeners.
3. Bathroom items such as scented and colored soaps, shampoo or bubble baths, hair spray, deodorants, makeup, flavored toothpaste, mouthwashes, lotion, and scented tissues.
4. Toys such as finger paints, play dough, colored chalks, glue, scented dolls, scented stickers, scratch-and-sniff books, pen or stamp dyes, felt tip pens.
5. Miscellaneous items such as gasoline or diesel fumes, paint fumes, scented candles, insecticides, and swimming pool chemicals.

As the reader can see, the food sensitive child can also breathe in or absorb through the skin many dyes and chemicals from ordinary household products. Our environment contains many chemical pollutants and synthetics that can adversely affect behavior. Parents must be alert to these and arrange the environment accordingly. Obviously, this is not a simple task. However, if it leads to improved behavior, most parents agree that it's worth the effort.

Shopping for Safe Foods

Shopping for safe food can be time consuming. Labels must be read carefully to determine whether the product contains unacceptable chemicals or additives. It should be stressed that careful reading of labels is essential. Manufacturers sometimes change their products and label the product as "improved." This can mean that new ingredients have been added, which might make the product unacceptable for ADHD children. Before making a product selection, it is wise to contact the local branch of the Feingold Association, which can provide lists of acceptable foods. In addition, the Feingold Association of the United States publishes a newsletter called *Pure Facts,* which provides information about individual products.

It should be emphasized that the list of ingredients found on packages or labels may not be complete. Sometimes manufacturers change the ingredients and continue to use the old label even though this practice is illegal. The Feingold Association, therefore, recommends the following:[12]

1. If there is doubt about the product, don't use it. Instead, find an acceptable substitute.
2. Whenever possible use fresh, unprocessed food instead of processed products.
3. If processed foods are used, obtain a current list of acceptable foods from the local branch of the Feingold Association.

The Feingold Association of the United States provides a number of other important shopping guidelines that should be considered when reading labels:[13]

1. Artificial color may also be listed as U.S. Certified Color, Certified Color, FDA approved synthetic color, or FD & C No. ———.
2. Artificial flavor might also be listed as flavoring, synthetic flavoring, smoke flavoring, or vanillin.
3. BHA or BHT may be hidden in Vitamin A, shortening, lard, beef and chicken fat, and chewing gum base.
4. Spices and natural flavoring may contain hidden salicylates. For example, carob may have orange flavoring added.
5. Oranges and red potatoes may be dyed, and therefore unacceptable.
6. The phrase "no preservatives added" can be misleading. The manufacturer may not have added a preservative. However, the supplier, from whom he purchased the product, may have used preservatives.
7. The phrase "100% Natural" or "Natural Ingredients" can be

deceptive. The word "natural" can apply to both acceptable and unacceptable ingredients. Therefore, it is important to read the label carefully.

8. Although fresh non-salicylate fruits and vegetables are generally acceptable, some may have a dyed peel or wax coating.

9. Fresh poultry, meat, and fish are usually acceptable. However, the purple meat inspection stamp must be removed before cooking.

10. As indicated previously, sugar can cause a child to react negatively. Therefore, the reduction of sugar intake is important. Sugar appears under a number of different names in processed foods. For example, brown sugar, molasses, honey, corn syrup, corn sweetener, fructose, sucrose, dextrose, and glucose are all sugar products.

11. In addition to careful food shopping, precautions must be taken in buying medicines, toiletries, and other household items. These also may contain artificial flavors and colors that can cause a negative reaction. Remember that the local branch of the Feingold Association, your pharmacist, or your physician can all be helpful sources of guidance in making purchases. In fact, the local branch of the Feingold Association can provide a list of medications that are compatible with the program.

Meal Planning and Preparation

Of course, meal planning and preparation takes time and effort. However, many family recipes can be acceptably altered by using safe substitute products. Again, the local branch of the Feingold Association may be able to provide a list of safe alternatives. Further, they may be able to provide recipes and menu plans that are compatible with your eating and cooking habits. *The Feingold Cookbook* is another excellent source. It contains a four-week menu plan and recipes for getting started. Once the shopping, planning, and preparation habits are established, the work will take less time. Also, the family will be eating more nutritious and better tasting food. Making the initial commitment and putting forth the required effort is most important. Parents who are willing to do this are usually able to implement the program successfully.

Involving Your Child in the Program

If your child chooses to eat the wrong food, a hyperactive reaction can occur quickly. Further, it can last for several days. In fact, two or three violations a week can result in the child being constantly overactive. Thus, close supervision and monitoring by the parents is important. However, no matter how closely a child is supervised, the youngster will frequently be placed in situations in which he or she may be tempted, encouraged, and even pressured to eat the wrong foods. It is, therefore, essential that parents make their youngster aware of the diet's purpose and the importance of sticking to it. The child himself must be committed to the program. Otherwise, he can undermine its potential effectiveness.

To encourage children to eat properly, I have found the following approach to be helpful. First, I talk directly with the child about those behaviors that are causing him or her to have difficulty at home and school. Most children are aware that they are behaving badly. If we discuss this with them in an understanding manner, they will often admit that they are having difficulty. I have found that many youngsters don't want to behave badly. They want to be successful. However, they are uncertain as to how to accomplish this goal. The goal, therefore, is to show the child that we want to help. By establishing a cooperative relationship with the child, it is more likely he or she will be a motivated, willing participant in the program.

The next step is to explain to the child that each person is born with a different brain, nervous system, and physical structure. None of us has any control over this. In other words, we cannot choose the kind of brain, nervous system, or physical structure we would like to have. However, this does not mean we have no control. Instead, we can learn how our body works and how to take care of it. One of the ways we care for our body is by feeding it good food. If we eat well, it is more likely we will feel good and behave better. On the other hand, if we fill our body with "junk," it is more likely we will feel bad and behave poorly. Thus, although there is nothing we can do about the body we inherit, we can do something about the way we care for ourselves. We can control the quantity and quality of the food we eat and this, in turn, can also help us to control how we feel and behave.

We can next explain to the child that even though he or she is physically similar to other children (has arms, legs, hands, eyes, ears, etc.), the youngster *is* different from them in one important way. He or she was born with a "sensitive nervous system," which reacts negatively to artificial foods and colors. When the child eats food containing these ingredients, his or her nervous system becomes upset. This causes the youngster to feel poorly and also to behave poorly. Several analogies can be helpful in explaining this cause and effect relationship to children. First, explain to the child that his or her nervous system is like a violin or guitar and has a number of strings that run throughout the body. When the strings of the violin become wound too tightly, the violin produces a loud, screeching sound. However, when the strings are adjusted properly, the music is pleasant to the ear. The child can make the strings of his or her nervous system too tight by eating the wrong foods. In other words, by putting artificial flavors and colors into his or her body, the youngster tightens the strings of his or her violin (nervous system) causing the child's behavior to get out of control. Eating the right foods, however, keeps the strings adjusted properly and helps him or her to behave well.

Another helpful example is to compare the nervous system to the lava in a volcano. Lava is the source of energy that keeps the volcano alive. However, when the lava becomes too hot, it boils over, destroying the land and its vegetation. When a child with a "sensitive nervous system" eats foods containing artificial foods and colors or chemical preservatives, this causes his or her "lava" to boil over. When the child reaches this point, he or she cannot maintain control and "boils over." It is, therefore, important for the youngster to eat the right foods. Safe foods enable the child to control his or her "lava" and make it a positive source of valuable energy. This helps the child to behave properly both at home and at school.

Once the child understands the importance of the diet, he or she can participate in the program in a variety of ways. For example, the youngster can work on the diary with his or her parents. This will help the child to see the differences in behavior as a result of eating appropriate and inappropriate foods. Parents can also take the child to the supermarket. He or she can be taught to differentiate between safe and unsafe products. The child can participate in reading labels and learn to distinguish between nutritious ingredients and those that are only concerned with taste and appearance. Such activities will make the child an active participant in understanding and controlling his or her own behavior.

The preceding examples point out to the child that unsafe products and ingredients can cause him or her to behave badly. Parents can use these methods to teach the youngster that he or she is responsible for making the right choices about eating food. In other words, by eating properly or improperly, the child chooses to be either in or out of control. As indicated in the previous chapter, acquiring an "internal locus of control" is important in helping each of us to achieve success. This program provides the child with the opportunity to learn that his or her behavior can be the direct result of the choices he or she makes.

One final point is worth mentioning. The child who is a willing participant in the program has the opportunity to learn to stand up for him or herself when others pressure the youngster to go off the diet. As we all know, acquiring assertive skills are a valuable asset in gaining control of our lives. Children on the Feingold program often find themselves in circumstances in which there are inappropriate foods (for example, the school cafeteria or at a birthday party at a friend's house). Parents should discuss these situations with their youngster. They can teach the child to make assertive statements such as: "I'm allergic to artificial colors and flavors and I can't eat that"; or "I can't eat foods with chemicals in them"; or "I'm very sensitive to those kinds of foods and can't eat them." Practicing such statements teaches the child how to cope with people who might encourage him or her to eat inappropriate foods.

Finally, parents can reward their child for staying on the diet and demonstrating good self-control. An example of a reward system is presented in Chapter 3.

Staying on the Diet Away from Home

There are a number of situations outside the home in which it is difficult to monitor the diet. Eating at a restaurant, Halloween and birthday parties, and eating at the school cafeteria can all pose problems. When eating at a restaurant, parents must ask questions about the food and its ingredients. Talking with the manager and explaining the family's needs might be helpful. It may be necessary to order only basic foods, such as fresh eggs, plain vegetables, or broiled meats. Sauces and other seasonings might have to be eliminated. Some families bring their own condiments with them.

When the child attends parties away from home, parents may have to plan ahead to ensure that diet violations do not occur. They may have to call the hostess to explain their child's special needs. Sending a substitute meal or snack might be helpful. At school, parents should ask the teacher to notify them about upcoming events so appropriate arrangements can be made. It is important for parents to explain the Feingold program (and how this affects the child's behavior) with the teacher. The teacher can help the child to control his or her eating habits at school. Further, the teacher can encourage good nutrition with all of the children in the class.

Diet vs. Medication

Implementing the Feingold diet requires time and effort. The difficulty of coping with food shopping and preparation is, at least initially, more time consuming and getting the child to cooperate can be formidable. Further, not all children improve their behavior using this program. However, my experience leads me to believe that the diet is certainly worth trying. Many children are sensitive to artificial colors, artificial flavors, and perservatives. They are overactive because they eat inappropriate foods. The Feingold diet avoids the immediate and unknown long-term side effects of medication. It avoids the psychological pitfalls as well and provides the child with nutritious, healthy meals. This can only be beneficial. Most importantly, however, the Feingold diet provides the child with the chance to control his or her own behavior. The child can use a natural method instead of taking medication. The child also has the opportunity to learn to control him or herself by making proper food choices. Thus, the youngster can take credit for progress instead of relying on stimulant medication.

One last point needs to be discussed. Many physicians, educators, and mental health professionals doubt the effectiveness of the Feingold diet. However, the Feingold program does work for many children. I believe it is certainly worth trying. Contact the Feingold Association of the United States to obtain the address and telephone number of the local branch, which provides support from parents who have had success with the diet. Further, shopping guides, recipes, food lists, a newsletter, and other projects that can help parents are also available.

Chapter 5

Teaching Sensible Thinking

The Importance of Sensible Thinking

The ADHD child usually has low self-esteem, an inability to cope with frustration, and a poor sense of self-control. Often the child does not stop to think. Frequently the youngster behaves impulsively, failing to direct his or her own actions. Such behavior naturally leads to feelings of incompetence. Hence, the ADHD child often has a poor self-image. A good self-image, on the other hand, is the result of learning to control one's actions. People who consistently behave well are often successful in coping with life's pressures.

As indicated earlier, the successful child has an "internal locus of control." Because the successful child believes that he or she is responsible for him or herself, there is less need to blame, distort, or to become defensive when receiving constructive criticism. This enables the youngster to better learn from others and to correct mistakes. Further, it makes it more likely that he or she will continue to perform successfully in the future.

The ADHD child usually does not have an "internal locus of control." Therefore the parents must train their ADHD child to think positively and to assume responsibility. They must help him or her to develop a sound, realistic philosophy. This is important because it will provide their youngster with an internal guide for dealing with life's challenges. However, as parents of ADHD children know, teaching their youngster can be especially hard. Because they don't think highly of themselves, ADHD children often expect to fail. As a result, they become defensive when criticized. Instead of listening and learning from their mistakes, they complain, blame others, or make excuses. They also tend to avoid challenging tasks. Typically, they take the path of least resistance. Unfortunately, this behavior only reinforces the ADHD child's view of him or herself as being a failure.

In order to break this cycle, parents need to train their youngster to think sensibly and productively. To begin, parents must first be aware of those mistaken beliefs that undermine the child's capacity to be successful. They must then help the child to replace these erroneous notions with a more realistic and productive philosophy. This will help the ADHD child to face and overcome challenges. Feelings of competence will follow.

Training for Sensible Thinking

In order to begin training the child to think sensibly, the parent can start by correcting the youngster when he or she misbehaves. This requires the following seven steps:

1. First, either ignore (if possible) or punish the behavior. This will stop it and bring it under control (See Chapter 7).

2. Wait until the child calms down and is ready to talk.

3. Point out how the child's faulty thinking (e.g., "my parents should always give me what I want") caused the child to become excessively emotional.

4. Point out how his or her excessive emotions led to poor behavior.

5. Identify a more realistic or productive way of viewing the situation (e.g., "parents are not here to just give you what you want. They are here to teach you to live wisely").

6. Demonstrate to the child how realistic, sensible thinking enables him or her to remain calm.

7. Discuss some better ways to cope with the situation.

The Child's Mistaken Views of Life

Each day there are a number of situations in which the youngster's faulty thinking can lead to poor behavior. Thus, there will be many opportunities for parents to put the preceding seven steps into practice. For example, consider the following which frequently occurs at meal time. Jeffrey complains bitterly when vegetables are served during dinner even though they are essential to a balanced diet. He claims he doesn't want to eat vegetables because he doesn't like them. Obviously, youngsters view vegetables quite differently than parents. Often children believe they must like food before having to eat it. If such a view goes unchallenged, it may lead to other mistaken ideas about life, such as "if I don't like it, I shouldn't have to do it" or "things should be the way I want them to be." Thus, his parents shouldn't make special meals for Jeffrey because he finds certain foods unpleasant. This would reinforce such faulty beliefs. It is far better to point out to Jeffrey that we eat certain foods because they are good for us. Further, we might then reward him for eating an appropriate portion of each item. The preferred foods could follow as a reward for eating vegetables or other food less preferred by the youngster.

Another good example in which faulty thinking interferes with the child's ability to achieve occurs in school. For example, children sometimes complain that they do not want to do school work because they do not like the teacher or the subject. Some children believe that if they don't like the teacher's personality or the subject matter, then complaining, procrastination, and the avoidance of work are acceptable. If parents allow the child not to do the work (because they believe "it puts too much pressure" on their youngster), this inadvertently supports the child's faulty view. If parents believe teachers and interesting subject matter are responsible for learning, they will unwittingly convey this attitude to their child. Thus, their youngster will look to external factors for motivation rather than relying on his or her own efforts and initiative.

We frequently hear children complain about those teachers who demand excellence. They believe that such teachers are "too hard" or "mean." It is important for children to learn that good teachers have high standards requiring their students to do their best. Striving for excellence is usually not easy. Many of us would probably agree that some of our most profound learning came from those adults who would not settle for substandard performance. As children we may not have liked these people. However, in retrospect, it was this insistence on excellence that may have enabled us to develop the skills and attitudes we have today. If we think further about this, how many of us would want our physicians to have taken only interesting courses and studied only with professors they found to be pleasant? Most of us would hardly be satisfied with this. Instead, we want our physicians to have the most rigorous training possible with the most competent professors. In fact, we want the same from doctors, lawyers, and teachers. Most of us want excellence, however, this cannot be attained with attitudes such as "I shouldn't have to do it if I don't like it," or "If I don't like someone, I shouldn't have to do what they ask or require." In fact, we must be willing to persevere at tasks that we find distasteful. We must learn to work with persons who would not necessarily win a popularity contest. The statement that learning and education should be fun is not always true. Learning is often difficult and demands much commitment and effort. If the child can learn this early in life, it is more likely he or she will acquire the self-control, persistence, and dedication that leads to maximum performance. This is not to say that some learning isn't actually fun and easy. Education is not always a painful experience. However, in most cases, subject matter is difficult and demanding. It is the parent's responsibility to help correct the faulty thinking that interferes with their child's ability to succed in life.

The Eleven Mistaken Views Children Hold

The main purpose of this chapter is twofold. The first is to help parents to identify the mistaken notions that children hold about life. The second is to present alternative, sensible beliefs for helping the child to become a responsible, achieving person. Let's begin by specifically focusing on those errors in thinking that interfere with the child's functioning.

The first mistaken belief: children believe they should like an activity before having to do it and if a task is difficult, their parents should take the unpleasantness away. How often do we observe youngsters who become resentful and even furious with parents who make them stick with something? Also, how often do we see parents become ambivalent and let the child "off the hook" when he or she is whining and fussing because of some difficulty? Some parents believe that requiring the child to complete difficult tasks creates too much pressure, which might "damage the child's psyche." Also, some parents believe that childhood should be a time in which there is an absence of hardship and accountability because we experience enough of this as adults. The youngster who is reared with this philosophy is not likely to develop those characteristics that will enable him or her to face challenges and to work toward satisfying long-term goals.

A colleague of mine told me a story about her mother who was an outstanding reading teacher. When the children complained about drinking orange juice, her mother would retort that one did not drink orange juice because one liked it. Rather, one drank orange juice because it contained vitamin C. My friend's mother challenged her children's mistaken belief and insisted they do what was best for them. If she had given in, she would have been reinforcing the children's mistaken view. As parents it is important to challenge the child's belief that responsibilities to self and others should be pleasant and easy. Parents need to encourage the child to engage in responsible behavior because it develops good habits leading to achievement in life.

The second mistaken belief: children believe that life should always be interesting and exciting. If boredom occurs, they believe it is their parent's responsibility to find fun activities for them. Such a faulty notion causes youngsters to be excessively dependent on their parents. Many children have a closet full of toys, games, and books. Still, they will often complain and whine because they are "bored." Unfortunately, some parents believe it is their responsibility to keep their children entertained. They constantly suggest and even arrange special activities for their youngsters. This only teaches children to look to others for stimulation. It prevents them from learning to rely on their own resources, which is essential for acquiring independence. As parents, therefore, our task is not to banish boredom from the child's life. Rather, we should alert the youngster to the curiosities and treasures that the world has to offer. During the early years, parents can make practical suggestions, such as calling a friend, riding your bike, reading a book, playing with your toys, and so on. It is then up to the child to make a choice. It is not a parent's responsibility to entertain the child or to take away boredom. The child must cope with this from the suggestions offered by the parents. If there is repeated whining and fussing parents can always present the youngster with the alternative of cleaning his or her room or performing some other chore around the house. Remember, if we want children to be independent problem solvers and to deal constructively with negative emotions (such as boredom), they must be encouraged to use their own (not their parent's) resources.

The third mistaken belief: children believe that life should be fair. Children often believe when something unfair happens, the situation should be immediately corrected to suit them. If the child does not learn early to cope effectively with the unfairness of life, then he or she may behave in a hostile, overly aggressive manner or just withdraw in the belief that there is no point in trying. Such reactions are a waste of valuable intellectual and emotional energy. How often do we hear children complain about something not being fair? Tantrums often result when they don't "get their way." The child must learn that life is filled with unfairness. For example, some talented individuals are able to perform an athletic feat with a minimum of effort, while others work diligently but fall short. Another common situation is when a child accidently breaks a valuable toy. Certainly the results of these situations are unfair and there may be no way to correct them. Therefore, the child must learn to come to grips with this fact if he or she is to adjust adequately. As parents, we want to make the lives of our children as painless as possible. However, it is learning to cope with frustration and disappointment that makes us strong. Judging ourselves to be a success or a failure in comparison with others and bemoaning life's unfairness often leads to dissatisfaction with self and the world. It is much better to judge ourselves using our own yardstick. In other words, teach your child to ask this question: Where did I begin and how far have I progressed? For example, the child who makes the baseball team through persistent effort and practice achieves more as a person than the talented youngster who makes the team easily. This child learns to overcome discouragement and frustration. Further, the youngster is building character traits that will serve him or her well in the future. It is important for parents to challenge the myth of fairness early in the child's life. Parents must teach the youngster to cope effectively with the realities of living. This will prevent negative emotions such as jealousy, resentment, bitterness, and hostility from interfering with the youngster's judgment. Further, it will free the child to use his or her intellectual energy for successful problem solving and the achievement of worthwhile goals.

The fourth mistaken belief: children often have the notion that their parents owe them things and that parents should give them what they want. If the parents also believe this, they will produce a child who is demanding, egocentric, and easily frustrated. As parents, it is important to point out to your children that parents do not owe them everything they want. What parents owe to their children are nutritious food, clothing, medical attention, a public school education, concern about their psychological well-being, and a reasonably comfortable home in which to live. Trips to the movies, the latest video game equipment, and so forth are luxuries. Parents give these luxuries to the child to make life more pleasant. However, the luxuries are not owed, nor are they essential to the development of worthwhile character traits. Further, when the extras of life are given to the child, parents expect reciprocation in the form of cooperation and responsibility. If this does not occur, feelings of resentment grow in the parent, which often results in a power struggle between parent and child. The parent berates the child for being "selfish," "irresponsible," "unappreciative," and so forth. The child claims the parent "is mean," "never listens," and "doesn't understand." It is important to keep in mind that over-indulged children are often not liked by peers and teachers. In fact, parents themselves frequently experience negative feelings toward over-indulged children. Moreover, the over-indulged child often does poorly in school and in other activities requiring persistence and concentrated effort. All this occurs because these children are used to getting things too easily.

Besides deficiencies in concentration and persistence, spoiled children exhibit another problem that hampers them in relating to others. They often fail to understand that reciprocation is essential in establishing effective human relationships. In my work with children, I encounter many youngsters who claim they love their pets, their parents, and their siblings. However, when I ask how I would know this, they are usually at a loss for words. At this point, I show them a plant in my office which I purposely water only occasionally so that it appears droopy and undernourished. I then ask them if I love this plant. The reply has always been "no." When I re-introduce the question of loving their pets that they "forget" to feed, or loving their parents whose requests are ignored, my point becomes much clearer. In essence, what I am attempting to teach the child is that if we care about or love something or somebody, we demonstrate this by our deeds. Following through on responsibilities to others shows we care about them. However, sometimes these responsibilities may be inconvenient or contrary to what we want to do at the moment. The child who learns that love requires commitment, effort, and the willingness to inconvenience him or herself for the betterment of others will be better equipped to function in the world. Such a child is more likely to be successful in relationships with others.

The fifth mistaken belief: children frequently hold the view that if they want something, they actually need it in order to be happy. Children often have very little patience. They can become overly frustrated or furious when a perceived need is not filled immediately. Parents reinforce this if they indulge their child by consistently giving him or her material items without requiring the youngster to exercise patience and a willingness to work. This results in a demanding child with a low frustration tolerance who cannot delay gratification or persist at challenging, difficult tasks. It is much better to teach children to distinguish between needs and wants so they don't become confused. The things we *need* are items that are necessary for survival and living reasonably well. The things we *want* are not necessary for survival. For example, video games, a television, or a stereo are not needed. They are extras that can make life pleasant; however, they do not necessarily lead to happiness nor to the development of character.

The sixth mistaken belief: children believe that adults should always follow through on promises regardless of circumstance. For example, a parent promises to take the child to a movie. However, some circumstance beyond their control prevents this from happening and the youngster has a tantrum insisting that the parent made a promise and must keep it. It is important for the child to learn that circumstances or events can sometimes alter plans. If the youngster does not learn to accept this, it only leads to unnecessary frustration. Parents must teach the child that nothing in life is guaranteed. There are some things that cannot be altered no matter how much we want them to be so. In other words, the child must learn to make the best of things, even when it is unpleasant or inconvenient.

The seventh mistaken belief: children believe that they must be first and should win all of the time. Adults are so competitive that we may unwittingly reinforce this faulty belief. It is better for the child to learn early that each person has strengths and limitations. It is more important for the child to learn "to do your best" not necessarily "to be the best." If we value ourselves only because we perform better than other people, we can become dissatisfied or unhappy. Most of us will never win all of the time. As mentioned previously, it is important we accept our strengths and weaknesses and develop ourselves accordingly. Each person begins at a different level and progresses at a different pace. Accepting this and learning to develop our own internal yardstick as a measure of progress leads to self-acceptance and satisfaction. Constantly comparing ourselves to others and being content only if we are superior to them leads to dissatisfaction over the long run.

The eighth mistaken belief: children often believe that making mistakes is bad. Often children believe that it is better to withdraw and not to take a chance rather than risk disapproval and failure. It is true that making mistakes is unpleasant. However, we can learn from our mistakes and use this knowledge to improve our performance. If one does not try, then learning and progress cannot occur. Parents must teach children to distinguish between *foolish* and *sensible* risks. A foolish risk would be one in which the child endangers life or limb with some daring act because others might call the youngster "chicken." A sensible risk, on the other hand, is one which can lead to some benefit regardless of the outcome. For example, the youngster who raises his or her hand in class to answer a teacher's question risks being wrong and that other children might snicker or laugh. However, the child who is willing to take such a chance might also get the recognition for being correct. Even if the answer is wrong, the youngster would still acquire the experience of speaking before the group. Further, he or she may obtain information leading to a correct answer the next time. In other words, by interacting in the class, this youngster can gain either way because he or she has been willing to try. This is a sensible risk. It can help the child acquire character traits that will enable him or her to cope successfully with life.

The ninth mistaken belief: children hold the notion that other youngsters must like or approve of them if they are to be happy. How often do we see children give in to peer pressure in order to obtain approval from the group? We are probably all familiar with children who would rather fail or not do as well as they could in school for fear they would be called "nerds." Youngsters who give in to this pressure prevent themselves from developing those internal, self-directed standards necessary for achieving success. Further, they become a slave to the opinions of others. In my work with children, I often point to the similarity between youngsters who give in to peer pressure and string puppets. If we allow other persons to "pull our strings" so to speak, then we actually give them control of our brain and our body. Most children can see that this is not desirable. They dislike the idea that they are allowing themselves to become puppets by giving control to others whose judgment is questionable at best.

It is much better to teach children to be individuals and to do what is right despite what other youngsters may think or do. A child needs much encouragement and support from his parents if he or she is to be successful in this regard. Parents must be diligent and make the child aware of proper values. If parents do not fill this void and educate their child properly, other less benign and sensible societal forces will do the job.

The tenth mistaken belief: children frequently believe that being criticized is bad and one must defend against it. How often do we hear youngsters argue back or ignore constructive criticism from an adult? Sometimes this occurs because parents are not skilled in giving criticism to their children. Often parents make global condemnations in which they accuse the child of being "totally irresponsible," "totally incompetent," or "always a pest." Instead, it would be better for parents to tell the child that they love him or her; however, they disapprove of some of the things he or she is doing. Then the parents should specifically point out those behaviors that bother them. In talking with their child it is important that parents keep their voices at a low, firm pitch and to clearly state that they are trying to help and not hurt the youngster. This will reduce the anxiety that the child may be experiencing. The message is therefore less likely to be met with denials and excuses. This will maximize the likelihood that the information will be received by the child so that an improvement in performance can follow.

The eleventh mistaken belief: children often believe that they "can't" do something. It is important that the child learn to distinguish between *can't* and *won't. Can't* means that one lacks the ability. *Won't* means that one refuses to exert the necessary effort even though the ability is present. In working with children it never ceases to amaze me how many youngsters say they can't do something. However, when I promise them candy or money to do what they say they can't, they work diligently and are often successful. Children must learn that believing they can't do something may be preventing them from being successful. The word *can't* is often self-defeating and leads to marginal performance and failure. Thus, it is important to challenge the child's erroneous view so the youngster doesn't underrate his potential for being successful in the future.

Comparison of Mistaken and Sensible Thinking

In summary the eleven mistaken beliefs and their rational counterparts are as follows:

faulty	*sensible*
1. I must like something or someone to be required to perform competently.	1. We don't have to like something or someone in order to perform competently. We do what is best because it is good for us, not because we like it or because someone pleases us.

2. Life should always be interesting. If I become bored or unhappy, my parents should be responsible for changing this.

2. The world is filled with interesting things and events. It is our responsibility to find and enjoy them.

3. If something unfair happens, it should be corrected immediately in my favor.

3. Life is not fair. Justice may not prevail even if we are right. There is no sense upsetting ourselves about things we cannot correct.

4. Parents owe children and should give them what they want.

4. Parents are not here simply to give children what they want. The parents' role is to teach the child to cope effectively with life and to provide the child with the wisdom they have acquired from their experience.

5. If I want something, I need it in order to be happy.

5. We must distinguish between wants and needs. Because we want something does not mean we need it. Wants are the extras in life. They are not necessary for survival or character development. Needs are things we must have in order to live reasonably well and to enhance the development of our character.

6. Adults should always keep promises regardless of circumstances.

6. Circumstances sometimes prevent adults from following through on promises. There is nothing one can do about this. Whining and fussing will not correct the situation or make it better. In fact, it just makes matters worse.

7. I must be first, and I should win all of the time.

7. It is better to do one's best rather than to try to be the best. It is more important to judge yourself by evaluating your own performance than by evaluating yourself in comparison to others.

8. Making mistakes is bad. It is better to not take a chance than to risk disapproval and failure.

8. Making mistakes can be beneficial. We can learn from mistakes provided we take sensible risks.

9. I must be approved of by my friends in order to be happy.

9. Use your own standards in making judgments about the important issues in life. Doing things simply to get approval from friends can cause you to lose your self-respect.

10. Being criticized is bad and I must ignore it or defend myself against it.

10. Criticism is valuable because it provides us with feedback. This can help us to improve our performance in the future.

11. If I say I can't do something, I really can't do it.

11. There are many things we can do if we put forth the necessary effort. In most cases we have the ability to perform successfully. However, we must be willing to try.

Parents must recognize that a sensible, realistic view of life can help the child to achieve. Faulty or mistaken assumptions cause discouragement, pessimism, and failure. Our beliefs about ourselves and others begin to form very early in life. If the child does not learn to think sensibly, he or she is likely to waste much intellectual and emotional energy making excuses and overreacting. This interferes with the ability to learn and to function successfully.

One final consideration should be taken into account in teaching your child to think logically and sensibly. In order to make good decisions, it is important to carefully weigh the pros and cons of each alternative. You should teach your child that every choice has both good and bad points. For example, most of us would agree that cigarette smoking is harmful to one's health. Yet people continue to engage in this habit because cigarette smoking produces some short-term pleasure even though the long-term effects may be disastrous. Thus, when your child argues with you about some course of action he or she wishes to pursue that you believe is not in the child's best interest (such as quitting school), acknowledge that it may have some positive aspects. The key however, is to get your youngster to look at the negative points as well. The following technique can be helpful. Take a sheet of paper and draw a line down the middle with a plus (+) sign over one column and a minus(−) sign over the other. You and your child should list all of the pros and cons in each of the respective columns before making a decision. This will help your youngster to sensibly examine all of the pluses and minuses associated with the choice before a decision is made. A sample decision sheet is presented below:

SHOULD I SMOKE?	
+	**−**
1. It will make me look older.	1. It leads to possible cancer and other health problems.
2. It keeps my hands busy.	2. It discolors my teeth and hands.
3. It helps me to relax when I'm nervous.	3. It causes my breath to smell bad.
4. It feels pleasant when I inhale.	4. It costs money.
5. It will help me to be accepted by my friends.	5. It's an addicting habit.

Chapter 6

Teaching Self-Control and Persistence

The Importance of Self-Control

Probably the most difficult task for parents of ADHD children is teaching them self-control. Self-control requires two things. First, the child must be able to avoid giving in to the temptation of avoiding responsibility. Second, the child must be able to structure his or her time, energy, and resources to satisfactorily complete projects within reasonable time limits. If we examine the characteristics of successfully achieving youngsters, we will usually find that they have enough self-control to complete their school work and chores at home on time. Thus, they do not have to make excuses for not getting things done. Further, usually such children do more than the required minimum. This results in a quality of performance far above the mediocrity with which their peers are often satisfied. Most importantly, these youngsters are able to maintain control over themselves and the use of their time. For example, they control how much TV they watch. By sensibly budgeting their TV viewing, they leave enough time for more important responsibilities. This same control is exercised in other areas of life as well. For example, the amount of time spent reading, talking on the telephone, playing with friends, and so forth is allotted on a sensible, priority basis. Thus, the lives of these children are usually well-ordered and goal-directed. As a result, they avoid the excuses used by their less self-disciplined peers.

Training for Self-Control

In this chapter our discussion focuses on how parents can help their child to develop self-control. Interestingly, in discussing "self-control," the importance of the *self* must be emphasized. This is where parents need to begin with the child. Parents must help the child to understand that the self has three parts: (1) intellectual, (2) emotional, and (3) behavioral. Further, parents must show the child how each of these contributes to his or her total functioning as a person. In order to do this, I have found it helpful to begin with a simple lesson in physiology. First, with regard to the intellectual and behavioral parts, I usually begin by talking about the brain. For example, I might ask the child to move his or her hand. Next I ask how he or she did this. Then we discuss how the brain sent a message to the hand telling it to move in a certain direction. I point out that the brain is the focal point of the body. It directs behavior by telling the arms, legs, or mouth what or what not to do.

To make the lesson even clearer, an illustration is provided. I draw an outline of a brain with buttons. I explain that pushing one of these buttons transmits messages through the nervous system to the various body parts. These messages direct our actions. Then I ask the child to engage in a few more behaviors such as standing, sitting, putting the right hand on the left arm, and so forth. We then talk about how the communication sent from the brain to the body parts resulted in certain behaviors. I also point out that the child may decide not to do these things. The brain might transmit a message such as, "Dr. Lavin wants me to put my left hand on my head, but I refuse to do it." Thus, despite my directives, this would result in the youngster doing something else or nothing at all. The critical point in this simple lesson is that the child has the control. By thinking correctly or pushing the proper "brain buttons," the child can make him or herself do or not do certain things. Thus, the rudiments of self-control are taught. This example teaches children that *they* can cause their own behavior.

In discussing the emotional aspect of self-control, a similar approach is used. First, I begin by teaching "feeling words," which describe emotions. It is important that the child learn the distinction between a feeling word and an opinion. Sometimes we make statements such as, "I feel like going to the movies," or "I feel that what he did was wrong and unfair." Such statements are not feeling words. They are opinions about something or an expression of what we want. Feeling words, on the other hand, convey our emotional reactions. They are words such as "anger," "hate," "nervous," "disappointment," "happy," and so forth. It is helpful to first make a list of such words with the child and to discuss the differences between them. This can be done by focusing upon the behavioral manifestations of each emotion. For example, in discussing "anxiety" you can point out that trembling, looking down, hand twisting, and blushing often occur when we are anxious. Also, you and your youngster could make a list of feeling words on a chart. The child might also cut out pictures from magazines to match them.

Once the child is knowledgeable about emotions, it is helpful to go back to our earlier discussion of the brain. We can now show how the messages from the brain influence our feelings about ourselves. For example, there are a number of messages the brain can deliver that would cause the child to be unhappy. These undermine confidence and the willingness to try to overcome challenges. Such messages would be statements such as the following:

1. I am stupid.
2. I always make mistakes.
3. There is no use trying. I'll fail anyway.
4. I might as well avoid work and have fun now because I'll mess up.
5. Other people are better than me.

If these "brain buttons" are "pushed" repeatedly, they will have a direct impact on how the child feels about him or herself. In other words, constant repetition of such statements will result in feelings of discouragement, depression, or self-pity. This occurs because the child believes he or she is incapable of being successful. Naturally, with such a view of self, this youngster would be more likely to watch TV rather than do homework. In addition, such a child would avoid responsibilities and instead be concerned with only having fun. Research on child development supports this. We know that a youngster's immediate emotional state influences his or her ability to resist temptation and to maintain self-control.[14] If a child is depressed, then he or she is more likely to give up rather than persist when challenged. On the other hand, if a child is happy and optimistic, there is a greater likelihood that he or she will continue to try to be successful. Thus, it is important to emphasize that there is a direct connection between what children learn to say about themselves and how they feel and behave. If a youngster repeatedly and consistently makes statements such as, "I am dumb," or "I can't do it," or "I'll probably mess up," he or she will feel depressed much of the time. Such a child will then behave like a discouraged person. This means the youngster will put off or avoid engaging in challenging tasks. In addition, the youngster will often whine and fuss when confronted with difficulty. This will be followed by excuses such as "I didn't have time" when responsibilities are not completed. Therefore, if parents want children to acquire self-control, it is important to teach them how to alter their mood states. This can be done by teaching them to replace negative self-statements with sensible sentences about their capacity to be successful. Thus, parents should instruct their child in making the following self-statements:

1. If I try, there is always a chance I can be successful. If I quit there is no chance.
2. I'm just like other people. I'm good at some things and I have difficulty with other things.
3. I am capable and can do what is required of me if I want to.
4. I can meet my responsibilities well if I put forth the necessary effort.
5. I have qualities that can help me to succeed with others.

Note that these statements are realistic rather than grandiose. Making statements such as, "I'm great," or "I'm better than everyone," or "Boy am I super," and so forth are usually exaggerations.

These can result in egocentricity and arrogance. In fact, many people who make such statements about themselves exaggerate in order to cover up their own sense of insecurity. Thus, it is important to teach the child to make self-statements that are realistic and positive. Discouragement and depression can be replaced with feelings of hope and confidence. This, in turn, leads to productive behaviors that enable the child to achieve successfully. The child who thinks, feels, and behaves positively will receive positive feedback from other people. This reinforces the good feelings the child has about him or herself. Further, it makes it even more likely he or she will display self-control in the future.

It is very important for parents to actually instruct their child in realistic, positive thinking. This will help the youngster to control his or her feelings and behavior. The research on child development has shown that teaching children to generate their own verbal instructions for dealing with situations requiring self-control can be beneficial, even at the pre-school level.[14,15] We all know that children are placed in a variety of situations in which there is great temptation to avoid responsibility. For example, the temptation to watch TV instead of doing homework is a common problem most parents face. Thus, it is essential to provide the youngster with instructions on how to cope with this impulse to avoid responsibility. First, parents must identify with the child those situations most likely to cause difficulty. Parents might discuss the pluses and minuses of doing or not doing homework as we mentioned in Chapter 5.

Parents can also work with the child to develop specific statements that the child can say to him or herself. These should help the child to immediately begin and to persist on tasks that are important to his or her development. For example, when the youngster comes home from school with assignments, the temptation to watch TV is a real problem. Thus, after identifying this situation as potential trouble, the following verbal instructions might be taught to your youngster: "As soon as I get into the house I will go immediately to my room and begin my homework. I will do it neatly and accurately and not allow myself to be distracted by the TV. If I do this, I will be showing self-control, which will please me and my parents." Note that in these statements, the verbal instructions emphasize *when* and *what* will be done ("As soon as I get into the house, I will go immediately to my room and begin my homework."); the *temptation* to be avoided ("and not allow myself to be distracted by the TV"); and the *consequences* for controlling oneself ("I will be showing self-control, which will please me and my parents.") These statements should help both to exert and maintain self-control.

For younger children of pre-school or early elementary school age, the sentences should be shortened to help them to retain the information. For example, let's suppose that the cookie jar is full of fresh baked cookies. You do not want your child to take the cookies without permission because eating them interferes with what he or she consumes at meal time. The verbal instructions you would teach would be as follows:

"I am not going to take cookies out of the cookie jar when I see it. I will be good and mommy and daddy will be happy." Note that these statements indicate *what* the child is going to do and *when* it is going to be done. Further, they indicate the *consequences* for behaving as expected.

The preceding examples provide the youngster with a verbal strategy for coping with a potentially stressful situation. In fact, parents can do the same for any situation requiring self-control. For example, sometimes youngsters are asked by peers for the answers to homework assignments. In order to be accepted, some children give up their work without thinking about the consequences. This occurs because they are too afraid to say "no," fearing they might be teased, ridiculed, or bullied. Parents can help their child to plan a strategy for dealing effectively with the temptation to give in. For example, if another youngster has a habit of asking your child for test answers, you might instruct your child to say, "I don't want to give the answers to John because it is the wrong thing to do." Have your youngster repeat this several times. Next, instruct the child on what he or she might say to John when he asks for the answers. Your youngster will then have a way to cope. For example, your child might say, "I don't want to give you the answers, John. It is the wrong thing to do and we might both get into trouble." By using this approach, your child will have a method for clearly controlling his or her behavior in dealing with this difficult situation.

Another factor that is important in helping children to develop self-control is teaching them to become aware of their own behavior. Psychologists call this "objective self-awareness."[16] In order to increase the child's objective awareness, it is helpful to distinguish between good self-control and poor self-control. This can be done by using games that teach the child to focus upon his or her behavior. For example, I sometimes present a youngster with a frustrating task such as untying a knotted shoestring or putting together a difficult puzzle. The task is potentially frustrating because a prize can be earned if it is completed within a short time limit. As the child is attempting the task, I try to clearly describe what he or she is doing that demonstrates self-control and good problem-solving skill. I then follow this with compliments such as, "Good, that's the way to stick with it" or "Excellent, you're trying a new approach since that one isn't working." If the child is becoming frustrated, I also attempt to describe those behaviors showing a loss of control. Further, I suggest the child calm down and try a different method. For example, I might say, "You're getting frustrated because you are repeating the same mistake again and again. Take a deep breath and tell yourself to calm down. Now try putting all the blue puzzle parts in one group and then match them with the green parts." By using this approach, parents can assist the child in three ways. First, they can help their child to identify the emotion interfering with his or her ability to think. Second, they can point out the inappropriate behavior causing the failure. Third, they can teach a new problem-solving strategy that would help their child to gain composure and be more successful. When the problem is completed, I ask the child to distinguish between those behaviors that demonstrate good frustration control and those behaviors that demonstrate poor frustration control. Such a technique increases the youngster's awareness of self. Also, it provides the youngster with specific behavioral strategies for maintaining self-control in future situations.

Another method I find helpful involves using a mirror. This allows the child to watch while he or she is both in- and out-of-control. In fact, after assigning a task to the child, I request that the child look at him or herself while working. We then contrast the appropriate and inappropriate behaviors at the conclusion of the exercise. Further, I sometimes ask the child to actually demonstrate good self-control and bad self-control while looking in the mirror. This usually heightens the youngster's self-awareness by making the contrasts between the behaviors even more vivid.

It is important to emphasize that parents must clearly describe to the child those behaviors that show good self-control and those behaviors that show poor self-control. It is often tempting to describe the child as "lazy," "irresponsible," or "immature" when he or she acts badly. It would be more beneficial to describe instead the inappropriate behavior ("Your materials are scattered on your desk, which causes you to be disorganized."), and then offer a better alternative. ("Place your books here. Put your papers in this area. Put your pencils in this container. This will make you better organized. Now you can work more quickly.")

One final point should be taken into account in helping your child to acquire self-control. As indicated earlier, the example parents set for the child is important in determining the kinds of character traits he or she develops. Children frequently emulate the behavior of their parents. This occurs because their parents are the most important people in their lives. Children therefore look to their parents for direction, guidance, and understanding. Thus, if parents show self-control, children are more likely to do the same.

In summary, to help ADHD children acquire self-control, it is essential parents teach them to make positive statements about themselves. The child who believes he or she is a capable person is more likely to be happy, optimistic, and confident. Further, such a youngster is more likely to acquire the self-control needed to be successful. On the other hand, the child who consistently makes negative statements about his or her capability is easily discouraged and depressed. Such a child is more likely to give up when challenged. Also, he or she is more likely to avoid responsibility and become self-indulgent. It is important to keep in mind that the verbal statements the child makes can affect the way the youngster feels about him or herself. People who believe positive, sensible things about themselves are happy and confident. People who have a negative, distorted view of themselves are depressed and pessimistic. Thus, it is essential that parents teach their children to make this connection as soon as possible. It is important for proper thinking habits and emotional control to develop early in life. Besides teaching sensible thinking, parents should help the child to develop an objective awareness of good self-control and poor self-control. This helps the youngster in learning to deal with frustrating situations. Further, teaching the child to give him or herself verbal instructions is helpful in maintaining self-control when he or she is tempted to avoid responsibilities. When the child does misbehave, we must remember to encourage the child and to teach him or her better strategies to be used next time. Parents might even rehearse or practice these with the youngster. He or she will be better prepared for a future challenge. Finally, it is most important that parents serve as good examples to their children. If parents exhibit self-control, then their youngsters are more likely to demonstrate this quality. This occurs because they look to significant adults for the guidance and wisdom that leads to responsible, successful living.

Chapter 7

The Use of Punishment: Learning from Mistakes

The Importance of Punishment

In Chapter 3 a brief discussion of punishment was presented as a method for curbing inappropriate behavior. Punishment is one of the foremost techniques used in child rearing. Thus, it is important for parents to implement it in a manner that will teach the youngster to examine the consequences of his or her behavior and to exercise better judgment in the future. It is essential to keep the following in mind. Punishment should be used to teach the child. Parents should not use punishment to get even for wrongdoings. If parents become overly upset about their child's behavior, more than likely they will lose their objectivity. This might cause them to engage in overkill. For example, sentencing Bobby to a two-month restriction for poor marks in school will not cause him to improve his grades. Rather, Bobby will more than likely just view his predicament as being hopeless. This often results in a youngster simply giving up or just continuing to perform poorly and learning "to live with less." How often do we hear parents say they "have taken away everything?" Nothing seems to work because their child "doesn't seem to care about anything." In most cases this is not true. Rather, the child has usually become discouraged and resentful. This often results in a power struggle, with the parents penalizing more and more and the child stoically adapting to less and less. In fact, some children will intentionally do poorly to "get even" with their parents. They are well aware that their failure pains their parents deeply. Such a cycle must be broken or the child will be wasting valuable intellectual and emotional energy that could be used for more productive purposes.

Whereas some parents resort to overkill, others are too lenient. They fail to punish when it is necessary. The child must learn early that failure to use good judgment leads to negative consequences. Unfortunately, many youngsters believe adults do not get punished in life. They think punishment is something reserved for children. It is important for the child to learn that negative consequences happen to everyone who uses bad judgment. In discussing punishment with your child, it is helpful to point out that parents also get penalized for inappropriate behavior. For example, if a parent is stopped by a policeman for going through a red light or for speeding, a fine must be paid by the parent. Further, if a parent is selfish and inconsiderate, that parent will not be liked by others. Moreover, you might point out that if mom and dad performed their jobs incompetently, they would lose their jobs. The family would then be without income. These are real punishments. In fact, the child should learn there are a number of rules that adults are required to follow. Violations of these rules lead to negative consequences. This helps children to understand that punishment follows for everyone who behaves badly. It is essential that a child realize early that punishment is to be expected for inappropriate behavior. It is unrealistic to expect rule violations and bad judgment to be rewarded or ignored. This is not a sensible approach to life.

Using Punishment Effectively

Punishment is an integral part of parenting. Thus, it is important that we formulate some sensible guidelines for penalizing appropriately. In order to formulate a good plan, we must first know the strengths and limitations of punishment. Punishment is something aversive. It is applied when the child engages in inappropriate behavior. For example, if Mary is using bad manners at the dinner table, we may take the food away and not allow her to eat. The purpose of this approach is to get Mary to stop what she is doing. In psychological jargon, we say the effects of punishment are primarily suppressive. In other words, punishment makes it more likely that an inappropriate or obnoxious behavior will not occur again. There are some important limitations to punishments, however. It does not teach the child how to behave appropriately. Rather, it merely inhibits unacceptable behavior. Therefore, punishment is limited in its effectiveness in child rearing. Although it has the advantage of stopping undesirable behavior immediately, punishment does not teach the child how to cope more successfully the next time. With this in mind, the discerning parent can see the advantages of using the material presented in Chapter 3, which is designed to teach the child to behave appropriately.

Three factors must be taken into account in administering punishment properly; the timing of the punishment; its intensity; and the quality of the parent-child relationship.[17] First, let's examine the timing of the punishment. In timing we are mainly concerned with *when* the actual punishment is administered. There is probably no factor that is more important in using punishment than proper timing. If a child behaves badly, it is essential that parents penalize the child as soon as possible. This makes a firm connection in the child's mind between the inappropriate behavior and the unpleasantness that followed. Thus, it is a poor punishment policy if the mother who gets angry with her child threatens the child with the statement, "Wait until your father comes home." Too much time elapses between the bad behavior and the delivery of the penalty. As a general rule, it is best to administer a mild punishment at the beginning of a bad behavior, while it is actually occurring or right after it happens. Some mild punishments might include: sending the child to a room for five or ten minutes; a verbal reprimand showing your disapproval of the behavior; taking away TV privileges; or requiring the child to perform some household chore. It should be kept in mind that any considerable delay between the inappropriate behavior and the punishment makes the punishment less effective. This occurs for two reasons. First, bad behavior can produce positive outcomes for the child in the short run. For example, when Jimmy throws a temper tantrum in the store and is "paid off" with candy as an appeasement, the candy may be very rewarding. Even though Jimmy is punished later, it may not be unpleasant enough to cancel out the earlier pleasure from the candy. Second, late punishment can be confusing to the young child. After Maggie breaks a rule, she may then behave appropriately for the rest of the day in hope of avoiding daddy's wrath later. In such a case, the punishment would actually be following good behavior. Ordinarily parents want to reinforce and encourage good behavior. Moreover, the child who is always severely punished by the father learns to fear him and to view the father as "the bad guy." This could hinder the development of the youngster's relationship with the father. Further, the child's negative feelings could interfere with his or her ability to learn from the father in the future.

Although timing is important, there are situations in which it may not be feasible to punish the child immediately. For example, if Randy is behaving badly in a store, at a friend's home, or while you are conducting a business transaction, the administration of punishment at that moment may not be possible. Thus, the punishment may have to wait. In fact, Randy's bad behavior may result in extra attention so that he can be quieted until more immediate tasks can be completed. In such instances, the punishment would obviously have to be delivered long after the inappropriate act. This is when the intensity of punishment becomes extremely important.

Research on child development has shown that punishment that cannot be delivered until later can still be effective. However, the youngster must view it as being sufficiently unpleasant. It is important to keep in mind that late punishment must still be related to the obnoxious act that occurred earlier. This makes the punishment meaningful and effective. Thus, before administering the penalty, the parents should point out the specific act that was in violation of the rules. The punishment must then be related to that act. It should be remembered that intense punishment does not mean beating the child. Rather, it means taking away some important privilege or requiring the child to perform some task demanding a high degree of physical or intellectual energy. Examples of the former would include taking away the use of the telephone, TV or bicycle for a week. Or perhaps requiring the child to go to bed one hour earlier each night. Examples of the latter would include requiring the child to write 100 sentences about what he or she should or should not do. Or performing extra chores around the house.

It is important for parents to know which punishments that your child will view as unpleasant. For example, parents might think that confining the youngster to his or her room every day after school for a week is an intense punishment. However, the child may view it only as a mild inconvenience because the child has a stereo, books, and games in the room to pass the time in a reasonably enjoyable fashion. In such a case, confinement of this nature would hardly be considered an intense punishment. It probably would not cancel out the rewarding aspects of having engaged in the obnoxious behavior earlier.

Finally, it is important to keep the following in mind. Sometimes parents know in advance that they will be taking the child into situations where there is a high likelihood of disruptive behavior. Parents should tell the youngster what is expected and what will occur if the rules are violated. Have the child then repeat back to the parents what the expectations will be and what will happen if rule violations occur. This allows you to be sure the youngster understands. If the youngster is confused and does not accurately repeat what you have said, clarify the situation once again. Thus, there will be no surprise if the punishment has to be administered later. One last point needs to be made. Don't make threats about punishments on which you cannot follow through. Telling your youngster you will "hang him by the heels" is an empty threat. The child usually recognizes this. In fact, many children view such punishments as meaningless since they know such things will not happen. Therefore, be sure you make sensible punishments that can be administered accordingly. This will provide you with the consistency and firmness necessary to obtain your child's respect.

The third factor that must be taken into account in using punishment effectively is your relationship with the child. Punishment is more effective if the child perceives you as nurturing and caring rather than as cold and distant. Thus, it is important to reward and praise your youngster generously when he or she performs appropriately. This will prevent the child from viewing you as a tyrant who is only interested in penalizing mistakes. As adults we must be cognizant of the fact that punishment is a powerful, but often overused tool. Since it often brings about immediate control, punishment is rewarding to parents. It is, therefore, tempting to use it again and again. Unfortunately, an overreliance on punishment may cause the child to be docile in your presence. However, the youngster often experiences considerable anxiety, resentment, and confusion even though he or she may say nothing to you. In the long run, such children can become fearful and unassertive with individuals they perceive as authority figures. A lack of assertiveness is not a desirable quality and prevents a child from learning to stand up for himself.

In addition to encouraging and nurturing your child, it is also important that you always explain to your child the reason for administering punishment. Research indicates that providing reasons for punishment increases its effectiveness.[18,19] However, it is important to keep in mind that long discussions are seldom effective in convincing the child that your punishment is correct. Rather, a short, right to the point explanation is more effective ("What you did was wrong. No ball playing is permitted in the house because you might break something.") Such an explanation makes it clear that the act violated a rule. The inappropriate act is also specifically identified. In addition, the possible consequences of the act are pointed out. There is a saying I often use with parents to try to sensitize them to a child's limited cognitive capacity for understanding long-winded adult reasons, "You can't pour thirty-year-old logic into a five-year-old head." In essence what this means is that adults have a lifetime of experience that far exceeds that of a child. When parents try to explain to their children all of the reasons for behaving sensibly now in preparation for the future, the explanations usually fall on deaf ears. This occurs because the child's living experience is limited. Children have difficulty in making the connection between what they do now and how this will affect them in the future. The child's thinking is limited to the here and now. Parents must reason and react to his or her behavior with this in mind. Therefore, a short, right to the point account of why the punishment is being administered is best. Also, it is important that punishment be followed with encouragement to try to do better the next time.

Another factor that must be kept in mind in administering punishment is whether you consistently set a good example for your child. For instance, some parents reprimand their child for using foul language. However, when they are frustrated, they say the very words the child is punished for using. Children are aware of these inconsistencies. They are quick to point them out to us. Further, such inconsistencies undermine the respect the child has for us. This can cause our punishments to be ineffective. Therefore, it is important that there is a consistency between what parents say and what parents do.

One final point should be taken into account about administering punishment. Parents must be careful not to follow punishment with affection. This may inadvertently strengthen the unacceptable behavior parents want to eliminate. Consider the following scenario. Molly behaves badly. The mother, who wants to be understanding and kind to her child, attempts to ignore the behavior. She hopes it will stop by itself. However, the behavior continues to worsen. The mother reaches the point where she cannot stand any more. She hits Molly in frustration. Molly wails and screams in pain. At this point mother feels guilty because she overreacted with her poor, defenseless daughter. She therefore atones by giving Molly an overdose of affection. She may even include a treat of some kind. Although this may help temporarily alleviate her guilt feelings, the same pattern usually returns. Molly behaves badly again. Mother tries to ignore the behavior. She attempts to be understanding, but then overreacts in frustration. This is followed by atonement and more bad behavior. In this scenario, Molly actually profits from her inappropriate actions that eventually lead to lots of affection or treats. The purpose of this example is to point out that punishment not delivered sensibly can have negative effects on both the parent and the child. Children who are periodically subjected to parental overreaction are likely to become confused and uncertain about behavioral limits. Parents who have no clear guidelines or punishment philosophy are doomed to inconsistency and haphazardness in their child rearing. When parents become prisoners of their own emotions, this prevents them from exercising good judgment in disciplining their youngster.

In summary, punishment can be an effective technique in child rearing if it is applied properly. Overkill and venting of rage are not effective methods of discipline. Overreacting does not help the child to distinguish between appropriate and inappropriate behavior. Punishment should be designed to teach a youngster that bad consequences follow inappropriate actions. This is a fact of life that applies to all of us. Thus, a punishment policy should be a sensible, planned approach based on psychological principles proven to be effective in child rearing. Timing, intensity, and the parent-child relationship are essential in the effective use of punishment. Punishment is most effective if it is delivered immediately. If it must be delayed, then the intensity of the punishment becomes a critical factor. This means that it must be sufficiently unpleasant to offset the rewarding aspects gained from engaging in the bad behavior. Further, the parent must be sure that the child understands that delayed punishment is being administered because of a specific inappropriate act that occurred earlier.

Four different factors must be kept in mind concerning the parent-child relationship and punishment. First, the child generally perceives the adult as a nurturing, caring person, the punishment will have a greater impact. Second, a short, right to the point explanation emphasizing why the inappropriate act was wrong makes the punishment more effective. Third, parental consistency is important. If parents make rules and then violate them by setting a bad example, the child will lose respect for them. Their reprimands and penalities will be rendered ineffective. Fourth, after punishment is administered, don't follow it with affection or special treats. This will lead to more undesirable behavior that the punishment is designed to stop. Finally, it should be stressed again that punishment does not teach the child to behave appropriately. Rather, it simply stops the child's bad behavior. Therefore, it is important that parents teach their children better ways of coping by rewarding and encouraging them whenever possible.

Chapter 8

The Use of Children's Stories: Teaching Good Planning Skills

The Use of Children's Literature

Helping the ADHD child to acquire good planning skills and better emotional controls is critical if he or she is to achieve successfully. Stories, fairy tales, and other forms of children's literature can be used to instruct youngsters in the principles of successful living. The advantage of using children's literature is that is appeals to the child's fantasy and imagination. Youngsters often identify with the characters portrayed in these stories and there are a number of excellent anecdotes and tales that parents can read to their children. Often these stories contain a moral emphasizing the importance of perseverance, courage, and the willingness to confront hardship and challenge in the pursuit of worthwhile goals. For example, all of us can remember the story, "The Tortoise and the Hare." By being diligent and persistent, the Tortoise won the race even when the odds were decidedly against him. How about the story, "The Little Engine That Could"? When confronted with climbing the steep and formidable hill, the Little Engine kept saying as he chugged, "I think I can, I think I can, I think I can." The Little Engine repeatedly kept delivering a sensible, positive message to himself. This increased his self-confidence and inspired him to overcome the challenge of the hill. If we think about it, the Little Engine was actually utilizing the self-instruction techniques discussed in Chapter 6. Another good story which teaches children the value of planning ahead, is "The Little Red Hen." As you might remember, it was the Little Red Hen who planted the wheat, harvested and milled it, and baked the bread. The goose, the cat, and the rat declined to help her and lazily frittered away their time. When the food was ready to eat, however, they received none. Doesn't a story like this convey the importance of using good judgment now in preparation for the future?

As the reader can see, the messages contained in various children's stories can be a valuable adjunct in helping youngsters to learn responsible, productive attitudes about life. Parents must remember that children have vivid imaginations and love to use them. This partly accounts for the success of many fast-food hamburger chains. They utilize comic characters appealing to the child's sense of fantasy. These attractive, humorous characters stimulate the child's imagination and youngsters are therefore more likely to want to purchase the chain's products. Younger children are likely to identify with "The Little Engine That Could" or with "The Tortoise and the Hare." However, older children might more readily identify and learn from biographies about sports, historical, or artistic heroes who have persevered and overcome various challenges. The point to keep in mind is that children until about the age of 11 or 12 are quite imaginative and fond of fantasy. Parents can take advantage of this by reading stories that convey a moral relating to achievement and responsibility. The following guidelines can be helpful in using children's literature:

1. Familiarize yourself with the various children's books at your local library. Ask your librarian to help you select stories stressing the importance of self-control, courage, persistence, and good judgment in coping with the problems of living.

2. It is important to select books appropriate to the age and maturity level of your child. Your librarian can also help you in making this decision.

3. After selecting your reading material, choose a time when you and your youngster can sit quietly without interference from

TV, playmates or other outside sources. You might even designate a "quiet time" during each day when you and your child can sit and read together.

4. Show your child the book and discuss the title and any illustrations on the cover. You might ask your youngster what he or she thinks the story will be about. This will stimulate the imagination by getting the child to think about what is going to happen.

5. Involve your child by discussing the pictures and how they relate to the story.

6. As you are reading, be sure to accent and alter the tone of your voice when you come to key words, phrases, and dialogue. This will make the story more lifelike and interesting to your child.

7. When the story is completed, summarize the important events with your youngster. Discuss the main characters and how they behaved. This will help your child to make sense out of what was just read.

8. After summarizing the story, discuss the lesson that was taught in the story. Help your child to formulate a moral such as, "If you keep trying like the Little Engine and tell yourself that you can, you will be able to do it" or "If you keep trying like the Turtle, you might win even though somebody else might think they are better than you."

9. Once the moral is formulated, discuss how your child might use it in his or her life. In fact, you or your youngster might bring up specific situations in which the moral can be applied. For example, you might focus on how the child could be like the Little Engine when he or she has to complete a difficult school assignment. Or you might discuss how the youngster could be like a Courageous Lion when he has to go to a new school or face a challenge for the first time. Thus, by using the moral and helping your youngster to identify with the main character, you are actually teaching the child to incorporate the message conveyed in the story into his or her thinking.

Use of Anecdotes Describing Irresponsible Behavior

Another technique that is helpful in teaching children to be responsible is the use of anecdotes describing youngsters who engage in inappropriate behavior. Some sample anecdotes for school age children are presented in Appendix C. These stories focus on a main character who acts irresponsibly. They describe the inappropriate behavior, the irrational thinking the character uses to feel better, and the resulting consequences of failing to plan ahead. At the conclusion of each anecdote, an analysis is presented. This will assist parents in understanding the dynamics of the story's content.

After reading a story to the child, the parents can discuss the main character's behavior, feelings, and the faulty thinking causing the problems. Both parents and child can then work together in proposing better ways of coping in these situations. In discussing the anecdotes with your child, the following questions can be addressed:

1. What situation or problem confronted the main character in the story?

2. How did the main character behave?

3. What were the results of the behavior?

4. What thoughts did the main character experience? How did the main character's thinking cause him or her to overreact and to behave poorly?

5. How could the main character have been more sensible in thinking about this situation? How would this have helped?

6. What better solutions to the problem might the main character have utilized? How should he or she have behaved?

7. If the main character had thought sensibly and behaved better, how might the outcome have been different?

These discussions will help the child to gain insight into the causes of inappropriate behavior. More importantly, it will teach the youngster to think and behave productively in dealing with problem situations. As indicated previously, such foresight and planning are the basis for successful achievement in life.

In conclusion, children have vivid imaginations and are strongly attracted to imaginary heroes. Thus, children's literature can be a valuable technique for teaching youngsters about life. Stories and anecdotes often convey a moral message. They can be used to teach children to think and to plan ahead in coping with life's problems. If parents take the time to select books wisely, they can use them to not only entertain their children, but to help them to live sensibly and productively.

Chapter 9

Successful School Performance

The Importance of Education

No book on the ADHD child would be complete without a chapter on education and the parent-teacher and child-teacher relationships in the school. Starting at the age of five or six, the child spends approximately six hours a day at school. During this time he or she is faced with a number of intellectual, social, and emotional challenges. Successful performance of these tasks is important if the child is to develop self-confidence and a positive attitude toward education and the future. Youngsters who do poorly in school and go on to become successful adults are the exception rather than the rule. Most youngsters who fall behind in reading, writing, and calculating skills in the early years do not simply "catch up" with the passage of time. Rather, they usually fall further and further behind. Also they develop a negative attitude toward school and learning. Moreover, instead of studying and working toward long-term goals, many of these children put forth a minimal amount of effort. They often spend their time in idle pursuits that are of little benefit in the long run.

In my work with ADHD children over the years, I have never met a parent who failed to recognize the importance of a good

93

education. However, I have met many discouraged parents who did not know how to motivate their children to study in preparation for the future. Further, I have worked with many parents of ADHD children who have just about given up on the schools. Many believed educators were insensitive to the needs of their child. Also, they contended that the schools could not or would not structure an appropriate program to help their youngster to learn successfully. It is no wonder, therefore, that many parents exhibit frustration resulting in a strained relationship between the home and the school.

Planning the Educational Environment

In this chapter emphasis is placed on discussing the educational environment. Also, recommendations are made for parents who want consistent feedback on their child's performance so they can reinforce what is being learned in the classroom. Before we get started, however, it is important to discuss the limitations of parents. First, parents are not teachers. Usually they are not expert in educating children in reading, writing, and calculating. Teachers attend a university for four years and study courses that provide them with an expertise in the field of education. Parents cannot gain such expertise by reading this chapter or a few supplementary books. Despite this limitation, however, there are contributions parents can make in the schools. For example, parents can become experts on their own ADHD youngster and those factors that motivate him or her. Further, by using "common sense" they can identify those behaviors that are prerequisites for learning in a classroom situation. As indicated in Chapter 3, the motivation of the ADHD child (or almost any child for that matter) is determined by what follows the youngster's behavior. Again, if pleasant consequences follow a behavior, that behavior is more likely to continue. If unpleasant or negative consequences follow, then the behavior is likely to terminate. This is a very simple, but basic law that serves as a guideline for understanding almost all human behavior. If it makes sense to use this approach at home, then it would be reasonable to expect that it be applied in school as well. The key, however, is to make sure it is implemented properly.

In working with teachers, I have occasionally encountered skeptics who claim behavior modification is not effective. They claim the program has failed to motivate or change the ADHD child with whom they have worked. However, further inquiry into the situation usually showed behavior modification was not at fault for the failure. Instead, poor management, improper use of punishment, not identifying appropriate rewards, or an inflexible school administration were responsible for the program's shortcoming. If we want to facilitate learning with ADHD children, the application of basic behavioral principles must be applied. Again, research shows that behavior modification, not drugs, is effective in improving academic achievement.[20] Thus, behaviors that are prerequisites to learning should be *clearly* specified and rewarded. Behaviors that detract from learning should be ignored or penalized.

With this in mind, it would therefore make sense that educators should be able to specify those behaviors that enhance or detract from the student's performance in the classroom. Moreover, these should be clearly communicated to the child. For example, specific instructions such as, "Sit in your chair with your feet on the floor and face the front of the room" or "Have your math book, pencil, paper and eraser on your desk" are more exact than, "Be good," or "Be more considerate." The latter instructions are often confusing to young children. However, the former instructions provide clear, specific behaviors that are more likely to facilitate learning in the classroom. Other sample behaviors that are prerequisites to effective learning in the classroom include:

1. Sit in the chair with feet on the floor; look at the teacher or the assigned learning task.
2. Have the proper materials on the desk for each lesson.
3. Complete class work neatly, accurately, and according to the instructions.
4. Complete homework neatly, accurately, and according to the instructions.
5. Enter and leave the room quietly.
6. Raise your hand before speaking; talk only when the teacher gives permission.

7. Begin assignments promptly.
8. Ask questions when you don't understand a lesson or assignment.
9. Listen and follow instructions the first time.
10. Organize books and materials neatly at your desk.

These are just some of the behaviors that must be required if the ADHD child is to attend to the task at hand. It is important to keep in mind that learning demands concentration. If a youngster has slovenly work habits and spends time fidgeting or looking around the room, it is highly unlikely that he or she will be a successful student. Further, if a child interrupts or is noisy and disruptive, then this detracts from the other students' learning as well. Thus, there are certain behaviors that ADHD students must engage in if they are to get the most out of a school situation. Parents want to be certain that their child is performing these behaviors appropriately. This helps the child to use his or her abilities to the fullest in the classroom and enhances prospects for the future.

As we discussed previously, it is important to encourage and reward responsible, achievement-oriented behavior if we want it to continue. The classroom teacher should also have a plan for reinforcing youngsters who behave as expected. Moreover, if a student fails to fulfill his or her responsibilities, a penalty should be applied based on the guidelines in Chapter 7. Some sample rewards for ADHD students to reinforce appropriate classroom behavior might include:

1. Reading a magazine or book.
2. Performing responsibilities (such as passing out papers, cleaning the board, etc.).
3. Carrying a message to the office.
4. Playing a game quietly.
5. Being first in line.
6. Using art materials.
7. Sending home a "good boy" or "good girl" note for the day.
8. Sending home a certificate for meritorious behavior in school for the day or week.

```
┌─────────────────────────────────┐
│     RESPONSIBLE BEHAVIOR         │
│        CERTIFICATE              │
│            TO                  │
│                                │
│   Name: _____        │
│                                │
│   Date: _____        │
│                                │
└─────────────────────────────────┘
```

9. Gold stars or stickers of any type.
10. A movie for the class.
11. No homework for that evening.
12. Extra recess or play time.
13. Listening to music or a story.
14. Statements of approval or praise
15. Free time
16. Assignment to a leadership position.

Another type of reward system that works well with young children is a picture of a "smilie face" with a word of praise and space for a name as in the following examples:

```
┌──────────┐  ┌──────────┐  ┌──────────┐  ┌──────────┐
│  WOW!    │  │  GREAT!  │  │  SUPER!  │  │ TERRIFIC!│
│          │  │          │  │          │  │          │
│Name: ___ │  │Name: ___ │  │Name: ___ │  │Name: ___ │
└──────────┘  └──────────┘  └──────────┘  └──────────┘
```

A child can write his or her name on the paper and deposit it in a jar. At the end of the week, the teacher might have a raffle in which three names are drawn. Each winner would receive a small prize (a candy bar or small trinket). Naturally, the more good behavior pictures a child receives, the more chances of winning a prize. As an aside, this technique also works well for parents who want their children to behave appropriately when the family takes a trip. Each time your child shows self-control, one of the good behavior pictures is awarded. These can be cashed in during the trip for a nickel each. The accumulated sum can then be spent at an arcade, an amusement park, or some other place children enjoy.

In addition to rewards for responsible behavior, penalties for irresponsibility must also be applied. Some sample punishments that might be used might include:

1. Isolation from the group.
2. Poor grades.
3. Sending the child to the office.
4. Calling the parents.
5. Having the child call the parents and report his or her misbehavior.
6. A note to the parents to be signed and returned.
7. Having the child write a note to the parents reporting the misconduct.
8. Loss of recess time.
9. Taking home incompleted work.
10. Write 100 sentences stating the responsibility that should be completed the next time.
11. A verbal reprimand.
12. Detention.

Remember, as the parent of an ADHD child, you will probably be working closely with the classroom teacher in monitoring your youngster's progress. Thus, any suggestions, comments, or assistance that you provide can make education a more viable process for your child.

Monitoring Your Child's School Performance

It is important for parents to get feedback from the school on a consistent basis. Consistent feedback will enable you to reward and penalize your child accordingly at home. Also, it will reinforce what the school is doing. This makes it more likely that your child will develop those skills necessary to achieve successfully. It may be necessary for the school to provide daily feedback on your child's behavior. A note at the end of the week or every few weeks is not satisfactory. Too much time passes between the time parents receive this feedback and the actual occurrence of the child's behavior. Remember, to increase or decrease behavior, rewards, and penalties must follow as closely as possible. Holding the child accountable every day makes it more likely that he or she will develop good behavioral habits. Once these habits have been developed and maintained for a period of time, then feedback from the school every few weeks would be appropriate. A daily checklist for the teacher to complete and forward to you might look like this sample:

Behaviors	Class	Class	Class	Class	Class
1. Begins work promptly	Yes ____ No ____	Yes ____ No ____	Yes ____ No ____	Yes ____ No ____	Yes ____ No ____
2. Has proper materials	Yes ____ No ____	Yes ____ No ____	Yes ____ No ____	Yes ____ No ____	Yes ____ No ____
3. Completes class work neatly & accurately	Yes ____ No ____	Yes ____ No ____	Yes ____ No ____	Yes ____ No ____	Yes ____ No ____
4. Completes home-work satisfactorily	Yes ____ No ____	Yes ____ No ____	Yes ____ No ____	Yes ____ No ____	Yes ____ No ____
5. Homework assign-ment. Write NONE if no homework					
6. Conduct rating for the day	Good __ Fair ____ Poor ____	Good __ Fair ____ Poor ____	Good __ Fair ____ Poor ____	Good __ Fair ____ Poor ____	Good __ Fair ____ Poor ____
7. Teacher signature					

It should only take the teacher a few seconds to fill in the checklist for each class. Little extra work is required on the teacher's part. However, you still obtain a considerable amount of information about your child's daily performance. In using this checklist with kindergarten and first grade students, "smilies" and "frownies" can be used instead of YES and NO. The teacher's signature should be required for each class to verify the accuracy of the information provided.

Once the program is put into effect, you can begin to reward and penalize your child for his or her performance at school. It is important to stress to your youngster that the checklist *must* come home. It must not become lost or misplaced because the child had a bad day. If you are using the program described in Chapter 3, one of the ways to earn a check or a "smilie" would be to bring the checklist home regardless of whether it was good or bad. This reinforces honesty and makes it more likely the checklist will come home each day. The failure to arrive with the checklist, however, would result in a "frownie" or minus going into the IRRESPONSI-BILITY or BABY BEHAVIORS column. Further, it might also mean the loss of play or TV privileges for the day. Thus, it would make sense for your youngster to make sure the checklist came home.

The next step is to devise a system for rewarding a good day in school. First, each YES the child receives would be one point. Each GOOD in conduct would be two points. Each FAIR in conduct would be one point. Of course, a NO or POOR would receive a zero. In the sample sheet provided the child could earn a total of thirty possible points for the day. We might then decide that 80 percent of the total possible points would be considered a good day (24 points in this example), 90 percent (27 points) would be an excellent day, and 100 percent (30 points) would be a super day. Anything less than 80 percent, however, would indicate that the child had a bad day that should not be rewarded. For 80 percent, the youngster might earn one small reward. For 90 percent two small rewards might be earned. A perfect checklist might earn three small rewards. Also, a weekly, bi-weekly, tri-weekly, and monthly schedule for 80, 90, or 95 percent of the possible total points might be devised as indicated in Chapter 3. This will encourage your youngster to maintain a solid performance over an extended period of time, which will firmly establish good work habits.

Another technique that might be helpful if the child is behaving poorly would involve a contingency contract. In this approach, a written agreement is made between the parents and the child.

The parents promise to deliver a reward if the youngster scores 80, 90, or 100 percent of the possible points from the checklist. A sample contingency contract might look like the example on page 101.

Note that in this sample a weekly format is used. However, the contract dates could be for a daily, bi-weekly, tri-weekly, or monthly period. Again, the 80, 90 and 100 percent rewards can be determined from the material in Chapter 3. This could also be written into the contract. Also, a penalty clause could be added to punish irresponsible behavior. For example, if the child "forgets" to bring home the checklist or does less than 80 percent for the week,

BEHAVIOR CONTRACT

Contract dates: _____ to _____
                    (beginning date)   (termination date)

Contractual parties _____   _____
                          (parent)   (child)

I _____ agree to the following in order to
        (child)

improve my performance in school.

If I score 80 percent on my school checklist then my parents will

_____ .
                    (reward)

If I score 90 percent on my school checklist then my parents will

_____ .
                    (reward)

If I score 100 percent on my school checklist then my parents will

_____ .
                    (reward)

Signatures

_____   _____
      (parent)   (parent)

_____
        (child)

_____
      (teacher)

penalties could be applied such as loss of play or TV privileges or "grounding" for the day or weekend. Finally, parents should try to type all contracts so that they look "official." This lets the child know that the agreement is a serious matter and not something put together at the last minute. When the contract is completed, all parties involved sign in the appropriate spaces. A copy should be given to the child so that he or she can refer to the terms of the agreement if necessary. This helps to eliminate excuses such as, "You didn't tell me" or "I forgot." Also note that there is space for the teacher's signature on the contract. By having the teacher sign the contract, it shows the child that both home and school are working together.

In summary, it is important for parents to attend to their ADHD child's educational progress in the school. This is where the youngster learns the academic and social skills that lead to successful achievement in the future years. Those children who work diligently at school will be better prepared for life's challenges. Parents are not necessarily experts in educational psychology, but they can become knowledgeable about motivating their own child. After reading the text, perceptive parents should have a basic understanding of human behavior that will help them recognize whether a classroom environment is arranged in a manner that facilitates academic learning and the development of responsible behavior. If the teacher has clearly defined expected student behaviors and has arranged appropriate reward and penalties, your child may prosper in this classroom. If this is not the case, then you will want to voice your concerns. It is important to keep in mind that if parents want ADHD children to behave appropriately, parents must reward their children on a consistent basis. This enables appropriate positive work habits to be developed and maintained. These do not develop by chance. Rather, sensible planning and both the home and the school working together can nurture it. If there are indications in the early years that your child is not performing as expected, it is important that daily school feedback be provided. This allows parents to reinforce what the school is doing by rewarding and penalizing appropriately at home. Holding the child accountable each day will make it more likely that he or she will develop the kind of work habits that lead to success. Accountability can be achieved by using a daily checklist that the child must bring home. If parents want to establish good work habits, feedback on the child's performance at school cannot wait for every two, three, or four weeks. This does not work because too much time elapses between the time of the behavior and the application of the consequences. However, once a consistent and responsible behavior pattern is established, weekly, bi-weekly, or monthly feedback will be enough to maintain your gains.

One final point is worthy of note. Parents might find the teacher to be resistant to the use of these behavioral approaches despite the fact the child is not performing as expected. If this is the case, parents should then seek out the advice and services of the school psychologist. If the school psychologist is too overburdened to respond quickly, parents should consider obtaining the services of a qualified private child psychologist. He or she could work with the school on the child's behalf. It is hoped that such extra assistance will not be needed. However, parents should be aware of and be prepared to use all available options. The child's education is an important priority. Finally, it is important to once again emphasize that parents and teachers must work together to train ADHD youngsters to be responsible, achieving persons. If both parties use sensible principles to guide and shape the ADHD child's behavior, then this goal can be achieved.

Chapter 10

Summary and Conclusions

What Is Needed

The purpose of this book is to emphasize that there are other methods besides drugs to help overactive children. Although these methods are not a "quick fix," they are safer and more effective in facilitating learning. Further, these techniques can train the ADHD child to acquire an "internal locus of control." Thus, the youngster can learn that he or she has the capability within to be successful. Relying on stimulant medication is a crutch that is often unnecessary. If the home and school environments are arranged appropriately, the ADHD child can learn without taking drugs. However, this is not easy. It requires that parents make a serious, concerted effort to truly help these problem children. We need better trained parents and professionals who understand ADHD children and how to work with them. In addition, smaller classes (even individual tutoring in some cases), the support of trained teacher assistants, proper classroom space and materials, and counseling services are other steps that can be taken.

The Controversy

Recently there has been much publicity indicating that Ritalin is an overused drug. However, some people will deny this. They contend that Ritalin is "cost effective" because it doesn't require the expenditure for the extra services mentioned above. These same people also contend that Ritalin is no more dangerous than aspirin. Let's examine these two points. Is it really "cost effective" to use a medication that simply calms a child? Ritalin does not teach academic skills; it does not teach self-control; and it does not enhance self-esteem. It may quiet the ADHD child. However, this does not solve the child's problems over the long run. I have seen a number of adolescents who were medicated as children. Unfortunately, medication was the only treatment that they had received. They were still poor students; they still had few, if any, friends; and they were still impulsive. However, now they were also committing anti-social acts as well. Because these youngsters had become a societal problem, they were finally getting the help that they should have received earlier. Is this "cost effective"?

With regard to the safety of Ritalin, let's make no bones about it. If Ritalin is so harmless, why is there such a controversy? An article in the August 1988 issue of *People* magazine highlighted a boy named Casey Jesson. According to his parents, Casey's behavior deteriorated after taking Ritalin. He had difficulty sleeping, lost his appetite, and began wetting the bed. In fact, Casey's behavior deteriorated so badly that even the doctor who prescribed Ritalin approved the parents' decision to take him off it. Of course, the school was opposed to this. They pressured the parents to continue with the medication. Mr. and Mrs. Jesson are now exploring other forms of treatment, but only after observing their son's deterioration following the use of Ritalin. The article goes on to point out that some children become violent, depressed, and even suicidal after being medicated. Does this sound like a drug that is as safe as aspirin? In the July 1988 issue of *Good Housekeeping* magazine, the article "The Ritalin Controversy Grows" appeared:

> For years the drug Ritalin has been prescribed to moderate the behavior of hyperactive children so they can learn. But has this potent drug come to be relied upon as a "quick fix" to quiet unruly children who *aren't* hyperactive? Many doctors, parents, and educators think so. The American Academy of Pediatrics believes Ritalin should be given to children *only as a last resort.*

And before it's prescribed, parents and teacher should try improving behavior in other ways, such as counseling, greater participation in physical-education programs, or even changing a child's seat in class.

Again, if Ritalin is so benign, why would the American Academy of Pediatrics take this position? Clearly, parents, educators, and physicians are coming to recognize that stimulant medication is not only overused, but that there may be better ways to help problem children.

Better Alternatives

Throughout this book, it has been stressed that there are a combination of approaches that can be used to help ADHD children to acquire better self-control. Medication is not the only alternative. For example, the child's nutritional habits may contribute to his behavior problems. The elimination of preservatives and artificial colors and flavors from the child's diet may help him or her to concentrate and behave better at home and school.

One of the best methods for helping ADHD children is the use of behavior modification. This approach rewards appropriate behavior with praise, attention, and even material items. Rewarding good behavior makes it more likely it will continue. In addition, parents must also penalize the child when he or she behaves poorly. It is hoped that this will help the youngster to recognize his or her mistakes and do better the next time. If parents consistently apply these principles, the ADHD child is more likely to learn self-control.

Although punishment is needed in working with ADHD children, it is important to keep the following in mind. Punishment does not teach the child how to behave. It merely stops the youngster from acting inappropriately. Thus, it is essential for parents to directly teach, encourage, and reward good behavior. This helps the youngster to develop coping skills that are useful in confronting life's problems. Applying punishment so that it does not impair the relationship with the child is important. Therefore, the punishment must be timed appropriately. Further, excessive punishment should be avoided. To ensure that your children will still view you as caring parents, encourage them to do better the next time. Avoid conveying an "I told you so" attitude. Remember, punishment is most likely to be effective if it is delivered by sensitive, concerned parents. The child is less likely to be defensive when he knows you have his or her best interest at heart.

In working with ADHD children, it is also important to help them to develop a sensible philosophy about life. If they learn to use their intellectual resources wisely, it is more likely they will be able to acquire better self-control. As we discussed earlier, ADHD children are impulsive. They do not stop and think. Rather, they take the path of least resistance. They tend to avoid responsibility without thinking of the long-term consequences of their actions. Thus, parents must correct the child's faulty ideas about life. They must help their child to weigh the pros and cons of his or her behavior. Further, it is important to teach children to be aware of what they think and feel and how this affects their actions. The child who knows how to cope is more likely to successfully face life's challenges.

Finally, most parents recognize the importance of education for successful achievement in life. Therefore, parents need to be aware of the child's classroom environment and whether their child is functioning and learning as expected. Although parents often do not have expertise in education, they can become knowledgeable about motivating their child. Further, they can assist the classroom teacher by holding their youngster accountable for the quality of work he or she produces. By rewarding and penalizing the child at home, parents are letting the youngster know they value education. Further, if the parents and the school both work together, it makes it more likely the child will acquire work habits to become academically successful.

One last point should be considered before closing. Parents serve as models to their children. By their example they teach many of the character traits and skills discussed in this book. If parents remember to keep this in mind, then it makes it more likely that their children will turn out to be responsible, successful adults.

Appendixes

The appendixes provide suggested readings for parents and lists of additional behaviors to be rewarded and penalized. Pertinent chapters are indicated in parentheses.

Appendix A — Sample of positive and negative self-statements *(Chapter 6)*

Appendix B — Sample of feeling words *(Chapter 6)*

Appendix C — Anecdotes for teaching children the effects of irresponsibility *(Chapter 8)*

Appendix D — Sample of responsible behaviors to be rewarded *(Chapter 3)*

Appendix E — Sample of irresponsible behaviors to be penalized *(Chapter 3)*

Appendix F — Sample of short-term or daily rewards *(Chapter 3)*

Appendix G — Sample of long-term rewards *(Chapter 3)*

Appendix H — Sample of encouraging and approval responses *(Chapter 3)*

Appendix I — Sample of mild and intense punishments *(Chapter 7)*

Appendix J — Further readings for parents

Appendix A

Sample of positive self-statements (Chapter 6)

1. I think I can do it.
2. I am capable of giving a good effort.
3. I can be a responsible person.
4. I'm still OK even if I make a mistake.
5. If I try I can be successful.
6. I can control myself if I work at it.
7. Even if I fail, I can always try again.
8. I can make things happen if I work at it.
9. If I keep working, I'll improve.
10. I'm capable of improving each time I try.

Sample of negative self-statements (Chapter 6)

1. I'm no good.
2. I'm stupid.
3. I'll fail anyway.
4. Everything I do is wrong.
5. I'm dumb.

6. There's no use trying because I'll fail.
7. I'm worthless.
8. Nobody could ever like me.
9. I always mess up.
10. I'll never do it right.

Appendix B

Sample of feeling words (Chapter 6)

1. Nervous
2. Anxious
3. Panic
4. Down
5. Disappointed
6. Depressed
7. Despair
8. Annoyed
9. Angry
10. Furious
11. Hateful
12. Jealous
13. Envious
14. Upset
15. Happy
16. Joyful
17. Sad
18. Elated
19. Uptight
20. Tense
21. Jittery
22. Jumpy
23. Confused
24. Uncertain
25. Frightened
26. Fearful

Appendix C

Anecdotes for teaching children the effects of irresponsible behavior (Chapter 8)

1. How Tom Avoids Responsibility

Tom, Larry, Bob, and Jim sit near each other in school. Last Wednesday Tom came in just before the beginning of class. He asked Larry if he could copy his homework paper in arithmetic. He told Larry that he had stayed up late the night before watching his favorite TV programs and he just didn't have time to complete the assignment. Larry was somewhat hesitant about giving Tom the paper. It had taken him over an hour to get all of the answers to the problems. He had missed several of the shows that Tom had seen because he wanted to get his homework in on time. It didn't seem right that Tom should copy his work and hand it in as his own. Also, if the correct and incorrect answers on both of their papers were the same Larry might not get credit for what he had completed. Besides, Tom was always pulling stunts like this. Every time he failed to complete his assignments, he would ask someone in the class if he could borrow their work.

A few weeks ago, Jim let Tom copy one of his papers. Both boys were given a zero by Mrs. Brown. The worst thing about it was that Tom wouldn't even own up to what he had done. Instead, he let Jim take the blame right along with him. No, Larry decided. He wasn't going to let Tom off the hook this time.

Larry looked at Tom and told him he wasn't going to give him the answers because he might get into trouble. Larry felt somewhat uncomfortable about doing this, but he wasn't going to let Tom put him on the spot this time. This kind of thing happened too frequently, and he decided he wasn't going to put up with it any longer.

Tom was really angry with Larry for refusing to give him the assignment. When Jim and Bob also refused to let him copy their work, he went back to his seat and plopped himself down in the chair. A confused look was on his face. "What the heck was the matter with those guys?" he muttered to himself. "I just didn't have time to get the work done. Don't they realize that I'd give them my paper if they needed it? What difference does arithmetic make anyway? I'm always having trouble with it. If I didn't copy it from someone, I'd never get the answers right. Don't those guys realize that people have to work together to help somebody who is having trouble?"

Analysis

This story indicates how Tom's cheating has alienated him from his peers. He refuses to give up TV to complete his assignments. Yet he expects his classmates to give him their work. Tom fails to realize that he has placed Larry, Bob, and Jim in a very difficult position. For these boys, it is hard to say no to a friend. However, they know that if they comply with Tom's request, they may lose credit for their work. The boys finally refuse. They become fed up with Tom's lack of consideration and the way that he takes advantage of them.

Tom can't understand why the boys will not give him the arithmetic assignment. At first, he is angry. When all of the boys refuse to give him the work, however, he becomes confused. At this point, Tom attempts to blame everyone but himself for his predicament. He blames the lack of time initially. Then he tries to make himself feel better by indicating that he would share his paper if the other boys needed it. Here Tom fails to acknowledge that he seldom has a paper to share. If he did, he wouldn't have to cheat. Next, Tom blames the subject matter for his difficulties. According to him, arithmetic is of no importance; therefore, it's not worthy of his efforts. Lastly, Tom reverts back to blaming his friends. He feels that it is their responsibility to solve his problem for him.

In discussing this anecdote, an attempt should be made to focus on how Tom's lack of consideration affected his classmates. Also, the faulty thinking he uses to keep from acknowledging his own lack of responsibility should be discussed. For example, Tom makes up excuses such as, "I just didn't have time to get the work done" and "What differences does arithmetic make anyway." Also, parents might focus on Tom's acknowledgment that he doesn't understand arithmetic and that he needs to copy the answers from someone to get them right. A strategy for dealing more effectively with this problem could be discussed.

2. Tony Loses His Temper

It was a cold, crisp fall afternoon. The boys from Cole and Springfield Elementary Schools were playing one of the big football games of the season. The score was tied six to six, and there were only a few minutes left to play.

Tony Jenkins was playing right end for Cole. For Tony, this had not been a particularly rewarding afternoon. He had dropped three passes that would have put his team in the position to score a game winning touchdown. Dropping the passes was only part of the problem, however. On two occasions, Tony cursed so loudly and stomped around so wildly that the referee had penalized his team fifteen yards for unsportsmanlike conduct. When Tony dropped the third pass, he became so unruly the referee threatened to throw him out of the game unless he calmed down. At this point, Wayne Philips, the Cole team captain, called a time-out to talk to his right end. He reminded Tony that the penalties were hurting the team. Wayne then told Tony to get ahold of himself. Wayne and the other boys were quite upset with his behavior. They knew that Tony was one of the best players on the team. However, when things didn't go his way, he just went to pieces. Wayne had even considered putting someone else at Tony's position. In fact, if things continued the way they were going, he had decided to do just that. After all, Tony's penalties were not doing the team any good. In fact, they could cost them the game.

With only a few minutes left to play, the situation looked good for the Cole players. They had recovered a fumble in Springfield's territory. In a series of running plays, Cole had moved the ball down to the Springfield seven yardline. When the boys came back into the huddle, Jim Robertson told Wayne that the right defensive halfback for Springfield was out of position. He indicated that a pass play might score a touchdown for Cole. Wayne knew Springfield wouldn't be expecting a pass. He told Tony to go down the field to the left and to run into the end zone. Cole broke from the huddle, and lined up for the play. This was Tony's big chance. This time he'd show them that those penalties didn't mean a darn thing. Once he scored, all of the bad things would be forgotten.

The ball was snapped to Wayne, and he went back to pass.

Tony ran to the left side of the field. The right halfback was out of position just as Jim had said. "This is going to be easy," Tony thought. Just as he crossed into the end zone, Wayne threw him the ball. The pass was right on the mark, and he reached up to grab it for the game winning touchdown. However, as he was preparing to make the catch, he tripped and fell to the ground. The ball went to his right and landed beside him. This was too much for Tony to take. He stood up and cursed as loudly as he could. Then he kicked the ball away from the playing field. At this point, the referee called a fifteen yard penalty on Cole for unsportsmanlike conduct. Now, instead of the ball being on the seven yardline, it was moved back to the twenty-two.

Fat chance of scoring now, thought Wayne Philips. Wayne then called a time-out. He told one of the new boys to come into the game at Tony's position. As Tony was leaving the field, he was mumbling under his breath. His head was down and both of his fists were clenched. "Why do things like this have to happen to me?" he thought. "I'm the best end on the team. They have no right to take me out of the game. It wasn't my fault that I tripped. What the heck is the matter with those guys anyway?" Just then the whistle blew. The game ended in a six to six tie. Cole moved the ball down to the Springfield twelve yardline on the next play but time had run out.

Analysis

Tony's failure to control his temper cost the Cole team a touchdown that prevents them from winning the football game. This story clearly indicates how one person's poor behavior can ruin a potentially good situation for other people.

Although Tony is respected for his athletic prowess, he only functions well when things are going his way. When he is frustrated, he erupts with anger. The more mistakes that Tony makes, the more tense be becomes. This mounting pressure reduces his ability to perform successfully. Eventually he is unable to function at all. This results in Wayne removing him from the game.

As Tony is leaving the field, he blames the situation and the team for his problems. Because he is one of the best players and because it wasn't his fault that he tripped, he feels that he should be allowed to stay in the game. Tony fails to realize, however, that if Cole had not drawn the fifteen-yard penalty, they would have beaten Springfield. After he leaves the game, Cole gains ten yards on the next play. If they had been on the seven yardline, this would have been enough to score a touchdown.

Of particular interest is Tony's inability to function when things are going against him. The irrational thinking that caused Tony to overreact should be discussed. Further, the effects of his behavior on others is also a worthwhile area for discussion.

3. Ron Does as He Pleases

"Boy, sometimes my mother really irritates me," Ron muttered as he got off of the bus. Ron's mom had told him to come straight home after school. The family had to go to Jamestown to meet Aunt Sally who was coming to visit them for the weekend. The plane wasn't arriving until five o'clock and Ron didn't see why he had to be home so early. Besides, the boys were getting together to play football after school, and Ron didn't want to miss the game. "I can always catch the four o'clock bus and get home in plenty of time for the family to get to the airport before Aunt Sally arrives," he said to himself as he walked into the school.

The more Ron thought about the situation, the angrier he became. By the time school ended, he had decided he was going to play in the football game. He would take the four o'clock bus in spite of what his mother had said. There wasn't any reason for coming home so early. He decided that he just wasn't going to obey his mother this time.

After leaving the school building, the boys gathered on the playground. It was a rough and tumble game, and the players on both sides wound up with soiled clothing, scuffed shoes, and dirty hands and faces. At ten minutes of four, Ron left the field so that he could catch the bus. His pants and shirt were covered with grass stains, and his hands, face, and hair were filthy.

When Ron got off the bus in front of his house, it was four-thirty. As he opened the door and went inside, he saw that his mother, his younger brother, and his sister were sitting at the table waiting for him. His mother had an angry look on her face. She gasped when she saw what he looked like. Ron started to protest when his mother scolded him for not coming straight home. He said they had plenty of time to get to the airport to pick up Aunt Sally. He didn't see why he should have to miss the football game. When his mother pointed out that it would take a half hour to pick up his father, Ron stopped talking and looked down at the floor. He shuffled his feet back and forth and mumbled a few things to himself.

When Ron's mother finished scolding him, he went to his room to get ready to leave. As he looked out the window, he noticed that the family was waiting for him in the car. "Why don't they just go without me," he said to himself. "How was I supposed to know that something like this was going to happen? Besides, why did Aunt Sally have to come to visit this weekend? I'd rather play football than see her anyway."

Analysis

In this story Ron's self-centeredness creates problems for the members of his family. Instead of complying with his mother's request, he arrives home late. When his mother confronts him, Ron attempts to defend his actions even though he knows that it was wrong to disobey her. Ron's behavior indicates that he feels guilty. However, instead of looking at his mother, he looks down at the floor, shuffles his feet back and forth, and mumbles to himself.

When Ron goes up to his room, he notices that his family is waiting for him. The statements he makes indicate he is angry and that he blames his family for the problem he has created. At this point, Ron refuses to acknowledge the responsibility for his behavior. Finally, he blames his Aunt Sally for the difficulty. This is the last defense he uses to protect himself from the guilt feelings he is experiencing.

In analyzing this story the importance of family responsibilities can be discussed. Ron's faulty thinking and how this prevented him from accepting the responsibility for his own actions should be other topics for discussion.

4. Jerry Chooses To Fail

Jerry decided that he just wasn't going to put up with it this time. He was sick and tired of doing arithmetic. When Mrs. Smith told the children to take out their math books, he sat upright in his chair and refused to move. "If I don't like something, I'm just not going to do it," Jerry said to himself as he glanced around the room.

Mrs. Smith and the children in the class had seen Jerry do this before. When he didn't feel like working on a subject, he would sit rigidly in his chair and refuse to do anything. At first, Mrs. Smith tried to get Jerry to complete his assignments, but now she just ignored him. A few of the children giggled when Jerry refused to work.

After the children took out their books, Mrs. Smith told them to turn to the unit test on page fifty-six and to complete the problems. She said that this would be the last grade that they would receive before report cards came out. She encouraged the children to try to do their best.

When Mrs. Smith mentioned the test, Jerry winced a little bit. He was caught in a dilemma. Jerry knew that he was barely passing arithmetic. If he received a failing grade on the unit examination, he might not pass for the term. Still, he didn't feel like working on arithmetic this morning. He wanted to show Mrs. Smith and the rest of the class that they couldn't make him do it. "What should I do?" Jerry asked himself. He knew if he brought home a failing arithmetic grade, his parents would really be upset. They might punish him for not passing. On the other hand, if he did the work, Mrs. Smith might think arithmetic was important to him after all.

Jerry stared at the board for a few minutes. When he first started refusing to work, it seemed that everyone was paying attention to him and encouraging him to do the assignments. Now nobody even cared. Instead of trying to help him, they just pretended not to notice him at all. Jerry looked around at all of the other youngsters in the room. They all had their books open and were working on the test. When he saw this he reached into his desk and took hold of his book. "What should I do?" he asked himself again. Finally Jerry decided that it just wasn't worth it. He released the book and put his hands back on the desk. "I won't do it," he muttered. "I'll show them that if I don't feel like doing something, I don't have to. Besides, they don't care whether I do the work anyway. What difference does it make?"

Analysis

Jerry's defiance creates problems for him at home and at school. Throughout the story, Jerry spends a good deal of his time trying to decide whether he will do the arithmetic test the teacher has assigned. The dilemma that he is confronted with is not an easy one to resolve. Jerry realizes that if he refuses to do the assignment, he will be punished by his parents. He also knows if he completes the work, he will be complying with the teacher's request. For some reason, Jerry does not want the teacher or the class to think they can influence his behavior.

An examination of this anecdote indicates one possible reason for Jerry's defiance. It might be that his defiance previously enabled him to get a good deal of attention. Initially when Jerry refused to work, the teacher and the other members of the class attended to this kind of behavior. Now they simply ignore him. It is evident that Jerry wants the approval of the teacher and the other youngsters. The statement, "Besides, they don't care whether I do the work anyway. What difference does it make?" suggests this. In analyzing this anecdote, Jerry's faulty beliefs ("If I don't like something, I shouldn't have to do it") should be discussed. Note how this caused him to make choices that are detrimental to him.

The importance of making good decisions should be focused on in discussing this anecdote. Throughout the story, it is evident that Jerry has failed to consider the consequences that will occur if he does not do the assignment. His failure to make the appropriate decision will not only result in a poor arithmetic grade, but it will also create difficulties for him with his parents. These results far outweigh the immediate advantages he might gain from not doing the work. How to make good decisions, and how our decisions can affect our lives now and in the future, might also be explored more fully in the analysis of this story.

5. Charlie Lets the Boys Down

"You just can't count on Charlie Peters to do the work," thought Robert as he was trying to decide which boys on the science committee should be assigned to the different projects. Robert's committee was attempting to build a full-scale model airplane so they could demonstrate the principles of aviation to the class. Each member of the group was responsible for building a part of the model and explaining how that part helped the plane to fly.

After the science period ended, Charlie had gone up to Robert. Charlie asked if he could be responsible for constructing the wings of the airplane. Building and assembling the wings would be a difficult job and no one else on the committee had volunteered to do it. In fact, Robert was considering doing the job himself. He knew this would be an important assignment, and he wanted to make sure it was done right.

Robert wanted to let Charlie build the wings. He knew Charlie was really good at making models. However, Charlie was the kind of a guy you just couldn't depend on. The assignment was due next week. If any one member of the committee failed to do his job, then the whole project would fall through. After deliberating for awhile, Robert decided to take a chance on Charlie. He went over to his desk and told Charlie he would give him the responsibility of making the wings. Charlie smiled when Robert gave him the assignment. He promised he would get the work done. He wouldn't let the committee down this time.

The boys decided they would meet the day before the project was due in order to assemble the pieces of the model. When the day arrived, however, Charlie had not completed his portion of the work. In fact, he had done almost nothing. That morning when it was time to get up to go to school, Charlie stayed in bed a few extra minutes thinking about the work he had not done. "How will I explain this to Robert?" he wondered aloud.

Charlie's stomach started to hurt and his head began to ache. "Why do I feel so awful?" he asked himself. His mother called him for breakfast and Charlie told her he felt sick and that he just couldn't go to school today. After examining him, Mrs. Peters decided Charlie had better stay home because he appeared to be quite upset. "A good day's rest will probably make him feel much better," she said.

As soon as his mother left the room, Charlie continued to think about how awful he felt. "No wonder I wasn't able to get the wings of the plane built," he said to himself. "Gosh, when a person feels this bad, he's lucky if he can do anything."

Analysis

It is evident that Charlie Peters is the kind of a person that is not dependable in class. As the story indicates, Charlie asked if he could build the wings of the airplane. Although Robert knew that Charlie was not very responsible, he decided to give him the opportunity to complete part of the group project.

The decision Robert made was a very important one. If Charlie failed to do the work, the assignment would not be completed on time, and the entire group would be held responsible. Robert knew this but he wanted to give Charlie the opportunity to prove himself.

For Charlie, this was a chance to show the teacher and the other members of the class that he could be counted on. He was given an important assignment. By completing it, he might have been able to change the other children's ideas about him.

Although Charlie was initially enthusiastic about the project, he did not do the assigned work. The results of this negligence are obvious. First, he has put Robert in a very difficult position because Robert was responsible for giving Charlie the assignment. Also, his behavior reinforces his classmate's past perceptions of him. They will continue to think of Charlie as irresponsible. Both of these areas might be focused on in analyzing this anecdote.

One other area might also be discussed. At the end of the story, Charlie tells his mother he doesn't feel well and he doesn't want to go to school. Later he indicates that being sick has kept him from completing the assignment. It is evident that Charlie is using this excuse to protect himself from the guilt feelings he is experiencing. Charlie knows he has not fulfilled his responsibilities to himself or to the other members of the group. However, it is difficult for him to openly acknowledge this fact. The excuses Charlie uses can be discussed in analyzing this anecdote.

6. The Failure

"What was the point of it all?" Mike wondered. "No matter how hard I try, it seems like I just never get any better in this game." For the last month, Mike had been practicing every day so he could make the baseball team. Today was the first day of practice. So far, it had been a disaster. He had struck out twice and had made two errors at second base. "If I make the team after this performance, it will be a miracle," Mike said to himself as he came trotting off of the field.

It was the last inning of the practice game. Mike was hoping that he would get the opportunity to bat once more. "Maybe I might get a hit and prove to the coach that I'm good enough to make the team," he said to himself as he was sitting on the bench.

There were five players who had to bat before Mike. That meant three of them had to get on base if he was going to get another chance to show that he was good enough for the team. Jim was up first, and he singled to right field. Tom followed with a double. The next two boys struck out, however. "Two outs," Mike muttered. "I'll really be lucky to bat now."

Robert Smith was the next batter. Robert had also struck out the first two times at bat. The boy who was pitching threw two quick strikes by Robert. However, the next pitch hit him on the back of the leg, and the umpire awarded Robert first base.

This was Mike's chance. The bases were loaded. If he could get a hit now, this would undo all of the mistakes he had made previously. Mike got up to the plate, and gripped the bat tightly. He just had to get a hit this time.

The first pitch was a high hard one on the inside corner. The umpire called strike one as the ball whizzed by Mike. "Oh great," Mike said to himself. "I just got up here, and already I've got a strike on me." The next pitch was a low one. Mike swung at it. This time he made contact, and the ball went far over the third baseman's head. At the last minute, however, the ball turned and it landed in foul territory by three feet. "Just my luck," Mike said to himself as he watched the foul ball. "That will probably never happen again." The next pitch came straight down the middle of the plate. Mike swung and missed it by a foot. "Strike three," the umpire shouted.

Mike just dropped the bat and walked back to the bench. A disgusted look was on his face. "That's it for me," Mike said. "I'm just no good at anything. There's no sense in coming back here tomorrow because I'll never make the team anyway. I guess I'll just stay at home from now on. That's one place where I won't have to worry about making a baseball team."

Analysis

Throughout this anecdote, Mike exhibits a self-defeating attitude. In each incident, he anticipates failure. Mike seems to think there is very little he can do to control the things that happen to him. The consistent references to his bad luck certainly suggest that he believes that the results will turn out poorly no matter what he does.

When Mike strikes out, he concludes he cannot do well in any of the things he attempts. As the final solution to the problem, he decides to withdraw from the situation completely. This is his last attempt to deal with the feelings of inadequacy he is experiencing.

In analyzing this story, an attempt should be made to determine how an individual's view of themselves can influence his or her behavior. People who see themselves as being competent often perform successfully; people who see themselves as being inadequate often perform poorly. The importance of making sensible statements about our ability to perform should be focused on in this story. How Mike "psyched himself out" of being successful should also be discussed. It is of interest to note that Mike failed to notice how well he hit the ball that went foul. Rather than view this as a positive indication of his ability, he instead downplayed his chances of doing it again. As a result, Mike's "self-fulfilling prophecy" became a reality.

7. Mary's Speech

It was almost time for Mary to give her report on the planets to the class. She had prepared a large chart showing how each of the planets revolved around the sun and how they compared with each other in size. Mary had been preparing the report for nearly two weeks. She knew a great deal about the subject. Whether she would be able to deliver her talk in front of the class was another matter, however.

Whenever Mary had to speak in front of the other children, she always became very upset. Even though she had done a good deal of work on her project, she did not want to have to present it to the class. Mary really disliked having to talk before the group. Her mouth got dry, her hands started shaking, and it felt like there were a million butterflies flying around in her stomach. "Waiting for Mrs. Simpson to call my name is like waiting for the end of the world," she said to herself.

Finally Mrs. Simpson called on Mary and asked her to present her material to the class. As soon as she heard Mrs. Simpson's voice, Mary's stomach felt like it was going to jump right out of her skin. She got up slowly and walked toward the front of the room. When she turned and looked at the other children, her face got red and her tongue felt like it was tied up in her mouth. When Mary started speaking, the words came out rapidly. Instead of looking at the class while she was talking, she glanced at the windows or walls. "If I have to look at the other children, I'll forget everything I have to say," she told herself.

After speaking about the planets for a few minutes, Mary looked at the class. She completely forgot everything she was going to talk about. For about thirty seconds, she just stood there without saying a word. The harder she tried to remember, the more she seemed to forget. "This is just hopeless," Mary thought. "I just can't think of what I'm supposed to say."

When Mrs. Simpson asked Mary some questions about the report, she was able to answer them very easily. She showed that she knew a great deal about the planets. After talking with Mary for a few minutes, Mrs. Simpson told her she could take her seat. As she was walking back to her desk, Mary felt relieved because the report was finished. When she started thinking about the situation, however, she began to realize that her speech had been the worst one in the class even though she knew the material very well. This depressed Mary. "What will I ever do if I have to go through this again?" she asked herself.

Analysis

In this story an attempt has been made to show how excessive anxiety can affect one's performance. Mary's physiological reactions and her behavioral manifestations indicate that she is having a very difficult time coping with the speaking situation. The dry mouth, the shaking hands, and the tightening in her stomach indicate Mary is extremely nervous. When she gets up in front of the class, her face flushes, she speaks rapidly, and she fails to make eye contact with the other children. Finally, Mary looks at the class and is unable to continue.

In analyzing this story, you and your child might try to identify those behaviors indicating that Mary is anxious. How it feels to be anxious and how to cope with anxiety might also be discussed.

One other point might also be examined in this anecdote. Although Mary felt relieved after leaving the speaking situation, she realized that her speech was a poor one because she was unable to communicate the material to the children in the class. Mary knows she would be confronted with similar situations later on. However, she doesn't know how she is going to be able to cope with them. At this point a discussion focusing on some things that Mary might do to solve her problem might be appropriate.

8. Barbara Loses the Election

It was almost time for the election of the homeroom representative to the student council. Barbara and Carla had both campaigned vigorously for the position, and the race was going to be a close one. Both girls had completed their final speeches and the balloting was getting ready to start. Mr. Richards passed out pieces of paper to the class with the names of the two girls and a box next to each name. Mr. Richards explained that the children were to indicate the candidate of their choice by putting an X in one of the two boxes.

Barbara was really nervous about the election. She had worked hard trying to convince the other youngsters in the class they should vote for her. She wanted to win badly. Barbara had a lot of good ideas for getting the students involved in the school program. If she was elected, she was sure she would be able to make the school a better place for all of the students.

After the children had marked their ballots, they brought them up and put them in a box in front of Mr. Richards' desk. When all of the votes had been counted the final results showed Carla was the winner. She received eighteen votes, and Barbara got ten votes.

After the results were announced, a number of the youngsters got up and went over to where Carla was sitting to congratulate her. Barbara did not get up from her seat, however. She sat rigidly in her chair and stared at the board where the results of the election were posted.

Barbara was both disappointed and angry about the outcome. She had worked extremely hard. She thought that she deserved to be elected the student representative. "I'll be darned if I'll go over to congratulate Carla," she said to herself. "I hope she does a lousy job representing the pupils in this class. That will teach them a lesson. Wait until they ask me to work with them on the class activities for the student council next week. I'll refuse to do anything. In fact, I don't think I'll bother to do anything for this class from now on."

Analysis

Barbara's disappointment and anger as a result of losing the election are clearly evident in this anecdote. When the other members of the class congratulate Carla on her victory, Barbara ignores her and the other members of the group. In fact, Barbara hopes that Carla will do a poor job of representing the class. If this occurs, she feels she will be somewhat vindicated for the disappointment she had experienced.

In order to really get even with the class, however, Barbara decides to take more direct action. She knows she has a good deal to offer in helping the class with their future activities. She believes that by withholding her services, she will be able to get her revenge. Apparently Barbara thinks this will upset the other children, and they will be sorry for not having selected her as the homeroom representative. She also thinks this will help to take away the frustration and hurt that she feels. Actually, this faulty view would increase her bitterness and resentment. Unfortunately, Barbara believes she should always win, and if she wants something, she should have it. Discuss the negative impact of such thoughts on Barbara's feelings and behavior. Also, it would be beneficial to talk about what is likely to happen if Barbara follows through on her bad decision. Then a more sensible course of action can be discussed.

9. Jill the Dreamer

It was almost time to leave school. Mr. Silvers, Jill's teacher, was giving the class the homework assignments for tomorrow's lessons. He assigned five pages of reading in social studies, a page of arithmetic problems, and a written spelling exercise. While Mr. Silvers was talking, Jill was looking out of the window. She was thinking about the things she was going to do when she left school. She hardly heard one word that Mr. Silvers said about the homework assignments.

The bell rang and the children started taking out the books they would have to take home with them. Mr. Silvers started passing out paper to the class and the children were putting it into their notebooks. Some of the youngsters were going to the closet to get their coats so they would be ready to leave the building on time.

In the midst of the activity, Jill suddenly realized it was time to go home. She noticed that the children had books piled on their desks, and they were getting ready to leave the school building. "What the heck is happening?" Jill wondered as she looked around at the other pupils in the class. She knew Mr. Silvers had assigned some homework. However, she couldn't remember what it was. Jill poked Ruth Thomas in the arm. She asked Ruth what the assignments were for tomorrow's classes. Ruth was putting on her coat and was in a hurry to get into the line. There was a kickball game after school. She didn't want to have to stop to go over the assignments with Jill. Just as Ruth got her coat on, she looked over at Jill and told her to ask Mr. Silvers about the homework. "Jill is always daydreaming," Ruth said to herself. "She hardly ever pays attention to what's going on. I'll be darned if I'm going to take the time to explain things to her."

Most of the children had gotten into line and were waiting to leave the building. Jill looked around in a confused manner. She didn't want to ask Mr. Silvers to explain the assignments again because Mr. Silvers would know that she had been daydreaming. She also knew that the children were in a hurry and they probably wouldn't take the time to help her. After thinking about the problem for a few seconds, Jill picked up three books and got into line with the rest of the youngsters. "To heck with the homework," she said to herself. "When I come into school tomorrow, I'll just tell Mr. Silvers I lost my paper on the bus, and that I couldn't do the assignments."

Analysis

As this anecdote indicates, Jill's daydreaming creates problems for her. Because Jill failed to pay attention in class, she was confused about the homework assignment. When she attempted to get the assignment from Ruth, Ruth refused to help her. Ruth didn't want to take the time to help someone who was always daydreaming. Apparently, the other children felt the same way since none of them would take the time to explain the assignment to her either.

The only alternative was to ask Mr. Silvers. Jill was reluctant to approach him, however, because she knew Mr. Silvers would find out that she had not been paying attention again. After deliberating for awhile, Jill decided to leave the building with the rest of the youngsters. The next day she planned to lie to Mr. Silvers so she could avoid being caught for her irresponsible behavior.

In analyzing this story, an attempt should be made to discuss Jill's decision and how this could affect her relationship with Mr. Silvers and the other children in the class. Suggestions for solving Jill's daydreaming can also be focused on in examining this anecdote.

10. Ann, the Absentminded

It was almost time to leave for school. Ann hurried to her room to get her coat and books so that she would catch the bus on time. Suddenly Ann remembered that a library book she had borrowed two weeks ago was due today. When she looked around her room, she was unable to find it anywhere. What made matters even worse was that her arithmetic and spelling books were also nowhere to be found. Ann was in a state of panic. "If I don't find the books soon, I'll miss the bus and I'll never get to school on time," she said as she rummaged around the room.

Finally Ann's mother decided to help her hunt for the missing books. As she entered the room, she scolded Ann for not putting things where she could find them. Ann complained that it wasn't her fault that the books were lost. "It always seems that things are never around when you need them," she said to herself as they looked around the room. After hunting for the materials for a few minutes, Ann's mother found the library book under her bed. When Ann saw where it was, she said she just couldn't understand how it ever got there. She said she thought she remembered putting it on the shelf next to her bureau.

The spelling and arithmetic books were still nowhere to be found. Finally Ann decided she would just have to go to school without them. As she was walking toward the front door, she noticed the two books were lying on an end table next to the divan. She rushed over to pick them up, ran out the door, and caught the bus just as it arrived at her house.

Ann was huffing and puffing as she got on the bus. She plopped herself down in one of the seats and breathed a sign of relief. "I just can't understand why I'm always having so much trouble finding my stuff," Ann said to herself. "It seems like things are never around when I need them." Just then she reached inside of her coat to take out her pen so she could finish an assignment that she had been working on. "Oh no," Ann moaned as she put her hand into her front pocket. "I forgot my pen and my pencil. Now I'll never be able to finish my homework on time. Why is it that things are always going against me?" she asked herself as she put her books down on the seat next to her.

Analysis

Ann's failure to put her books and other material in a place where she can find them results in a good deal of difficulty for her. When Ann is confronted by her mother, she blames everything but herself for her predicament. In this way, she attempts to avoid the responsibility for her behavior.

Apparently Ann's absentmindedness extends to her homework assignments as well. Although there is no indication that she forgot to do the assignment, she put it off until the last minute. As a result, she was unable to do it because she did not bring her pen and pencil with her. This is another indication of Ann's failure to organize herself properly.

In analyzing this anecdote, a discussion of how Ann might cope with her problem more effectively would certainly be appropriate. Also, an analysis of Ann's tendency to blame other things for her difficulties should be explored. As long as Ann continues to not accept the blame, she will be unable to develop a constructive plan for solving her problem.

Appendix D

Sample of responsible (or "Big Boy" or "Big Girl") behaviors to be rewarded (Chapter 3)

1. Ready for school on time
2. Comb hair
3. Wash hands and face
4. Take bath
5. Brush teeth
6. Do homework neatly and accurately
7. Clean room
8. Make bed
9. Pick up toys
10. Feed pets
11. Set table
12. Wash dishes
13. Take out trash
14. Vacuum rugs
15. Weed garden
16. Cut the grass
17. Rake leaves
18. Home for meals on time

19. Wash and clean automobile
20. Eat all food on plate
21. Carry groceries
22. Do what is asked the first time
23. Read a book
24. Practice piano, dancing, gymnastics, etc.
25. Turn out lights when finished
26. Sharing with brother, sister, peers
27. Good table manners
28. Saying "please" and "thank you"

Appendix E

Sample of irresponsible (or "Baby")
behaviors to be penalized (Chapter 3)

1. Lying
2. Stealing
3. Cheating
4. Late for dinner
5. Forgetting
6. Not turning out lights
7. Poor table manners
8. Temper tantrums
9. Interrupting
10. Back talk
11. Cursing
12. Not doing what is asked after a reminder
13. Yelling
14. Failure to obey
15. Playing ball in the house
16. Running in the house
17. Teasing
18. Hitting others

19. Breaking things
20. Not completing homework
21. Arguing
22. Behaving poorly at school
23. Whining and fussing
24. Failure to do assigned chores
25. Not ready for school on time
26. Fighting with siblings
27. Throwing things
28. Borrowing without permission
29. Not putting away toys

Appendix F

Sample of short-term or daily rewards
(Chapter 3)

1. Use of TV
2. Use of radio
3. Use of video game
4. Use of stereo
5. Snacks (chips, popcorn, candy, ice cream, cake, cookies, etc.)
6. Coke or other soft drink
7. Ride bike
8. Use of telephone
9. Stay up extra half-hour
10. Watch TV special
11. Go to library
12. Play game with parent
13. Have parent read a story
14. Take walk or go for a ride with parent
15. Have a friend over to play
16. Have a special dessert
17. Help mom make dinner
18. Visit a friend
19. Draw, paint, or make crafts
20. Read to parent

Appendix G

Sample of long-term (weekly, bi-weekly, monthly) rewards (Chapter 3)

1. Go to fast-food restaurant
2. Go to a more expensive restaurant
3. Go out for ice cream sundae
4. Have a friend stay overnight
5. Go to a friend's house overnight
6. Go out for pizza
7. Order a special meal at home
8. Roller skating
9. Ice skating
10. Movie
11. Buy a record
12. Buy a $5 toy
13. Fishing ·
14. Go to baseball or football game
15. Go to amusement park
16. Picnic
17. Go camping
18. Visit grandparents for weekend

19. Buy clothes
20. Go swimming
21. Take friend with you to a movie, ballgame, restaurant, etc.
22. Stay up late for the weekend
23. Go to arcade
24. Buy a video game cartridge
25. Take a day trip to place of child's choice

Appendix H

Sample of encouraging and approval responses (Chapter 3)

1. Excellent piece of work.
2. Good, keep plugging.
3. That's the way to work at it.
4. Nice effort.
5. Keep working. You're making progress.
6. That's outstanding.
7. Super. That's the way to do it.
8. Your fine work pleases me.
9. That was very creative.
10. Good thinking.
11. You should be proud of your effort.
12. That's a marked improvement.
13. That's a better way to go about it.
14. I'm proud of your work.
15. I appreciate your good work.
16. Keep trying.
17. Don't give up. You can do it.
18. That was a good decision. It shows thought.

19. You certainly showed that you could do it.
20. You're showing a really positive attitude.
21. Your work is both neat and correct.
22. That was especially well done.
23. You're doing fine. Keep at it.
24. That's the best you've ever done.
25. You deserve a gold star for that effort.
26. You really kept your cool that time.
27. Fantastic effort.
28. Beautiful work.
29. Fabulous.
30. Go ahead. You're going in the right direction.
31. That's right on target.
32. That shows a good deal of thought.
33. Terrific work.

Appendix I

Sample of mild punishments (Chapter 7)

1. Take away TV, radio, video game, and telephone privileges for the day
2. Confinement to room for 10, 15, 20 minutes
3. Do a chore that takes 30 minutes
4. Loss of play time for the afternoon
5. Loss of bike riding privilege
6. Eating alone
7. "Grounded" for part or all of the day
8. Apologizing for bad behavior
9. Go to bed half hour earlier
10. Loss of bedtime in 10-minute increments for each rule violation

Sample of intense punishments (Chapter 7)

1. "Grounded" for the weekend
2. Loss of TV, radio, and telephone privileges for the week
3. Writing 100 sentences about how to behave appropriately the next time

4. Go to bed 1 hour earlier every day for a week
5. Doing a chore (or chores) to pay back for rule violations plus an extra chore for causing inconvenience
6. Staying in the house after school every day for a week
7. No friends visit for a week
8. Loss of use of toys, bike, etc. for a week
9. Confinement to room for the weekend
10. Write a letter of apology and deliver it in person

Appendix J

Further readings for parents

Alvord, J. *Home Token Economy*. Champaign, IL: Research Press, 1977.

Bartz, W. R. & Rasor, R. A. *Surviving with Kids: A Lifeline for Overwhelmed Parents*. San Luis Obispo, CA: Impact Publishers, 1978.

De Risi, W. & Butz, G. *Writing Behavioral Contracts*. Champaign, IL Research Press, 1975.

Dinkmeyer, D. *Systematic Training for Effective Parenting: Parent's Handbook*. Circle Pines, MN: American Guidance Service, 1976.

Eimers, R. & Aitchison, R. *Effective Parents/Responsible Children*. New York: McGraw-Hill, 1978.

Feingold, Benjamin F. *Why your child is hyperactive*. New York: Random House, 1975.

Homme, L. *How to Use Contingency Contracting in the Classroom*. Champaign, IL: Research Press, 1971.

Krumboltz, J. & Krumboltz, H. *Changing Children's Behavior*. Englewood Cliffs, NJ: Prentice-Hall, 1972.

Lavin, P. *Teaching Children to Cope*. Annapolis, MD, Board Co., 1980.

Madsen, C. & Madsen, C. *Parents Children Discipline: A Positive Approach*. Boston: Allyn & Bacon, 1972.

Madsen, C. & Madsen, C. *Teaching Discipline*. Boston: Allyn & Bacon, 1970.

McGuinness, Diane. *When Children Don't Learn.* New York: Basic Books, 1985.

Patterson, G. *Living with Children.* Champaign, IL.: Research Press, 1975.

Taylor, John F. *The Hyperactive Child and the Family.* New York: Everest House, 1980.

Zifferblatt, S. M. *Improving Study and Homework Behaviors.* Champaign, IL: Research Press, 1970.

References

1. McGuinness, D. When Children Don't Learn. New York: Basic Books, 1985.

2. Byrd, D. P. and Byrd, K. E. Drugs, Academic Achievement and Hyperactive Children. The School Counselor, 1986, 33, 5, 323–331.

3. McGuinness, D. When Children Don't Learn. New York: Basic Books, 1985.

4. Byrd, D. P. and Byrd K. E. Drugs, Academic Achievement and Hyperactive Children. The School Counselor, 1986, 33, 5, 323–331.

5. Seligman, L. Helplessness. San Francisco: Freeman, 1975.

6. Crandall, V. Katkovsky, W. and Crandall, V. J. Children's beliefs in their own control of reinforcements in intellectual-academic situations. Child Development, 1965, 36, 90–109.

7. Gagne, E. The effects of locus of control and goal setting on persistence at a learning task. Child Study Journal, 1975, 5, 193–199.

8. Byrd, D. P. and Byrd, K. E. Drugs, Academic Achievement and Hyperactive Children. The School Counselor, 1986, 33, 5, 323–331.

9. McGuiness, D. When Children Don't Learn. New York: Basic Books, 1985.

10. The Finegold Handbook. Alexandria, VA: The Finegold Association of America, 1983.

11. The Finegold Handbook. Alexandria, VA: The Finegold Association of America, 1983.

12. The Finegold Handbook. Alexandria, VA: The Finegold Association of America, 1983.

13. The Finegold Handbook. Alexandria, VA: The Finegold Association of America, 1983.

14. Fry, P. S. Affect and resistance to temptation. Developmental Psychology, 1975, 11, 466–472.

15. Hartig M. and Kanfer, F. H. The role of verbal-instruction in children's resistance to temptation. Journal of Personality and Social Psychology, 1973, 25, 259–267.

16. Liebert, R. M. and Nelson, R. W. Developmental Psychology. Englewood Cliffs, NJ: Prentice-Hall, 1981, 422–423.

17. Liebert, R. M. and Nelson, R. W. Developmental Psychology. Englewood Cliffs, NJ: Prentice-Hall, 1981, 167–170.

18. Teizer, V. I. and Rogers, R. W. Effects of methods of discipline, timing of punishment, and timing of test on resistance to temptation. Child Development, 1974, 45, 790–793.

19. Liebert, R. M. and Nelson, R. W. Developmental Psychology. Englewood Cliffs, NJ: Prentice-Hall, 1981, 418–419.

20. Rumain, B. Efficacy of behavior management versus methylphenidate in a hyperactive child: the role of dynamics. American Journal of Orthopsychiatry, 1988, 58, 3, 466–469.

Index

153